The Trial of Jesus

Simon Légasse

SCM PRESS LTD

Translated by John Bowden from the French *Le Procès de Jésus, L'histoire*, published 1994 by Les Éditions du Cerf, Paris.

0 334 02679 2

First published 1997 by
SCM Press Ltd
9–17 St Albans Place London N 1 0NX

Typeset at The Spartan Press,
Lymington, Hants

Printed in Great Britain by
Biddles Ltd,
Guildford and King's Lynn

Contents

Contents

Introduction

Nowadays, pessimism tends to set in among scholars who approach the question of the trial of Jesus. First, if we are to believe some of them, the sources at our disposal provide only a paltry historical residue. Moreover, it is noted that this scanty material takes on different contours, depending on the choices made and the hypotheses put forward. This can only darken the prospects and discourage new undertakings from the start. It is true that the way in which the subject is tackled and the disciplines used in treating it affect the results.

First, confessional preoccupations, both Jewish and Christian, often interfere in this sphere and jeopardize the freedom of enquiry, whether because of an apologetic concern to reduce the part of the Jews in this affair or because people are afraid to apply the strict rules of literary and historical criticism to the Gospel accounts.

Two works have made their mark on the research of the last thirty years, both of which illustrate these two obstacles well. The first is that of the Jew Paul Winter,[1] whose thesis goes as follows. Accepting that at that time the Sanhedrin had the power to execute those who had been condemned, had Jesus been judged and condemned by the Jewish tribunal, he should have been stoned. But he suffered crucifixion, which was a Roman punishment. So it was not the Jews who condemned him, but the Romans. They organized and carried through the whole trial, making use of Sadducean hierarchs, and executed Jesus as a political agitator. The Romans took the initiative in the affair and brought it to a conclusion. However, while recognizing that the tendency of the evangelists is generally to diminish the responsibility of the Romans and blame the Jews, one has to face what is indicated by a faithful study of the texts: Jesus was certainly arrested on the initiative and on the order of the Jewish authorities, and then handed over by them to the justice of Pilate.

The second is that of Joseph Blinzler, a Catholic exegete, whose *The Trial of Jesus* was first published in 1951. An English translation appeared in 1959.[2] The author, whose learning is faultless, dispenses with literary criticism of the Gospels or even any investigation of the views of their authors. In short, everything is historical and if there are inconsistencies between one piece of evidence and another, a little good will is enough to remove them. So John mentions only an appearance before Annas and no hearing by the Sanhedrin as the Synoptics do? That doesn't matter: one can call the first session a 'preliminary interrogation' , seeing the passage set in the house of Caiphas, who is hardly mentioned in John 18.24, as preparing evidence for the Sanhedrin session, which John will not have thought worth reporting, since this had been done by the Synoptics and moreover it was not interesting to pagan Christian readers. The nocturnal judgment by the Sanhedrin does not raise the shadow of a doubt, nor does its course as reported in the Synoptic Gospels, though this needs serious critical study. For Blinzler, the Roman trial according to John, in which John in fact presents his own theology, proves an accurate tradition, if not to the letter, at least in substance,[3] and thus supplements the Synoptic Gospels. These examples, which could be multiplied, leave a painful impression: a reader accustomed in any way to historical methods comes up against an idiosyncratic view, unable to free itself from the blinkers which prevent it from looking reality in the face or at least raising the real questions.

While making use of these works and numerous others, in this brief study I want to avoid several traps.

One would be to relegate the Gospel accounts of the passion to the realm of pious legend with no historical substance. In reality these accounts embroider a basic tradition; this tradition has certainly been rearranged, but its origin is to be put in the circle of the first witnesses to the events. So the use of the Gospels is imperative, all the more so since they are the only documents to *relate* the course of events to us in detail. To refrain from using them would be as wrong-headed as to neglect the Acts of the Apostles in attempting a biography of Paul. The important thing is to proceed by making use of the tools of a healthy literary and historical criticism, and also to seek to penetrate the intentions and the share of each author in the presentation of facts.

A second trap is to favour the contribution of law, Jewish or Roman, in the seeking to understand the trial. Certainly it is indispensable here to draw on the best sources, and that is what I have tried to do. But not to the point of being slave to a perspective which claims to be be able to explain everything. Rather, a collaboration between exegetes and historians of the law is to be favoured. This has quite considerable advantages. If, for example, the exegete succeeds in proving that the trial of Jesus before the Sanhedrin, a process duly culminating in a death sentence according to the two Gospels of Mark and Matthew, is a fiction inspired by theology and polemic, it is a waste of time for the historian of law to try to resolve the legal problems inherent in this episode. Another place where this collaboration is useful is in the case of the audience before Pilate, the course of which is steeped in themes indicating the involvement of a Christian pen; this only gives a slight idea, if any at all, of what really could have happened. In this case the legal specialist, instead of getting deeply involved in the Gospel texts, is all the freer to describe on the basis of this knowledge what he thinks most likely to have happened.

In no way do I claim to be definitive, nor do I want to disguise the element of uncertainty which must attach itself to this subject. But I believe that at the end of our study we shall have discovered the main outlines of this affair, and, given its often painful impact on the story of one part of humanity, it is useful to discuss it and write about it again.

I

The Sources

We have two categories of sources for the trial and execution of Jesus, non-Christian and Christian.

Non-Christian sources

We have no document from the imperial archives relating to the trial of Jesus, and despite the allegations of certain church fathers,[1] there is no evidence that any document was preserved in Rome. *The Memoirs of Pilate*, an abusive document that the anti-Christian emperor Maximin II Daia promulgated in 311 or 312, putting it up in poster form and disseminating it in the schools, is a false manifesto which, if we are to believe Eusebius,[2] was wrong about the date of the crucifixion: it fixed the crucifixion in the seventh year of Tiberius, or 21 CE, whereas Pilate only arrived in Judaea in 26.

By contrast, other facts deserve more than a simple mention. First comes the testimony of Flavius Josephus, who finished his *Jewish Antiquities* (= *Antt.*) in Rome in 93–94. Book XVIII contains the famous notice about Jesus:

About this time there lived Jesus, a wise man, *if indeed one ought to call him a man*. For he was one who wrought surprising feats and was a leader of such people as accept the truth gladly. He won over many Jews and many of the Greeks. *He was the Christ*. When Pilate, upon hearing him accused by men of the highest standing among us, had condemned him to be crucified, those who had in the first place come to love him did not give up their affection for him. On the third day he appeared to them restored to life, for the prophets of God had prophesied these and countless other marvellous things about him. And the tribe of the Christians, so-called after him, has still to this day not disappeared.[3]

The general authenticity of this text can hardly be disputed, and is so less and less today: Josephus elsewhere attests his knowledge of the Christian movement and its founder;[4] the language and style are not enough to establish the intervention of a foreign hand. Discussions begin when we ask how far this text has been glossed by a Christian. Despite the reservations of certain scholars, it is difficult not to recognize a Christian pen in the two phrases in italic in the quotation.[5] It is in fact hard to see how a Jew could contest that the word 'man' was enough to describe Jesus. The phrase 'He was the Christ' (*ho Christos houtos ên*) is quite redundant because of the term *Christianoi* which follows:[6] rather, this statement, which interrupts the course of the narrative, will have been introduced into the text after having been a marginal gloss, something which happens often in palaeography.

For our purposes it is enough here to note from the Jewish historian that Jesus was condemned by Pontius Pilate and crucified on the 'indication' or 'denunciation'[7] of the leaders of the Jewish nation.

Some years after the redaction of the *Jewish Antiquities*, Tacitus, in his *Annals* (XV, 44), written around 100, reports the reprisals in which the Christians were the victims, following the burning of Rome. Nero

fastened the guilt and inflicted the most exquisite tortures on a class hated for their abominations, called Christians by the populace. *Christus, from whom the name had its origin, suffered the extreme penalty during the reign of Tiberius at the hands of one of our procurators, Pontius Pilate*, and a deadly superstition, thus checked for the moment, again broke out not only in Judaea, the first source of the evil, but also at Rome (*per urbem*), where all things hideous and shameful from every part of the world meet and become popular. Accordingly, an arrest was first made of all who confessed; then, upon their information, an immense multitude was convicted, not so much of the crime of arson, as of hatred of the human race.[8]

The passage in italics seems to be an insertion deriving from some revision, but all scholars regard it as the work of Tacitus. The question arises as to the sources of his information. If we exclude the official register – 'it is hard to see . . . how the Roman registers could have attached Pilate to the name of Christ, far less to that of Christians'[9] – and if we rule out direct contact between Tacitus and the Christians, everything is hypothetical, including the possible use of the *Jewish Antiquities*.[10] Although Josephus was highly esteemed in Rome,[11] and Tacitus could have used the *Jewish War*, a document of unique importance, 'it seems very unlikely that Tacitus, who had the most profound contempt for Judaism, would have searched the *Jewish Antiquities* to find something to complete his narrative of the fire of Rome'.[12]

Be this as it may, apart from the explicit dating of the death of Jesus under Tiberius, Tacitus does not add anything to Josephus' testimony; he even falls short of this, since he omits any participation of the Jews in the affair, and consequently does not give a reason for it.

By contrast, this reason is indicated, and the Jews are incriminated, in a curious document which was published for the first time in 1855,[13] a letter which a certain Mara bar Serapion, a Syrian Stoic, wrote to his son studying at Edessa. Here is the passage which is of more particular interest to us:

What good did it do the Athenians to kill Socrates, for which deed they were punished with famine and pestilence? What did it avail the Samians to burn Pythagoras, since their country was entirely buried under sand in one moment? Or what did it avail the Jews to crucify their wise king, since their kingdom was taken away from them from that time on? God justly avenged these three wise men. The Athenians died of famine, the Samians were flooded by the sea, the Jews were slaughtered and driven from their kingdom, everywhere living in the dispersion. Socrates is not dead, thanks to Plato; nor

Pythagoras, because of Hera's statue. Nor is the wise king, because of the new law which he has given.[14]

Unfortunately the date of this letter is uncertain. The high dating which puts it only a few years after the destruction of Jerusalem in 70 is opposed by that which sees it as a work from the second half of the second century or even the middle or the end of the third. The mention in the letter of the deportation of the inhabitants of Samosata to Seleucia, Mara being among the exiles, is in fact an argument that can be used in both directions. One can envisage the flight of Antiochus, king of Commagene, of which Samosata was the capital, with his wife and children, when Cesennius Pactus, governor of Syria, advanced to occupy the city on the orders of Vespasian;[15] this took place in 73 and indisputably had consequences for the population of the city. But we also know according to the stele of Shabhur I at Naqsh-i-Rousten that following the defeat of Valerian in June 260, Samosata was occupied by the Sassanid army, which would have resulted in a deportation of the supporters of the Romans. Whether it dates from the second half of the third century or two centuries earlier, Mara's letter seems to derive its information either from Christians or from Jews who had themselves been informed by Christians, given the total silence over the role, essential though it was, of the Roman governor in the affair of Jesus and the attribution of his death to the Jews alone. However, the echo of the title of 'king of the Jews' suggests rather a Christian source of information, while the supposed sympathy of the philosopher for the Romans against the Persians could have been the motive for his silence over the role of the former. But we must also take account of the literary and didactic need for a parallelism between the three cases listed, which would have resulted in making Jesus the victim of his own people.

It is again to the Jews that a note in the Talmud attributes the execution of Jesus:

On the eve of the Passover Jesus (Yeshû) the Nazarene was hanged. A crier had gone before him for forty days, saying: 'Here is Jesus the Nazarene, who is to be stoned because he has practised sorcery and led Israel astray. Let all those who know anything in his defence come and plead for him.' But no one was found to take his defence, and he was so hanged on the eve of the passover.[16]

This *baraita* certainly relates to Jesus of Nazareth and not, as has been claimed, to another Jesus, disciple of R.Joshua ben Perahyah, who would have lived a century earlier, in the time of the king Alexander Jannaeus.[17] The addition 'the Nazarene' (*ha-Nosri*), which leaves no doubt about his person, is very well attested. Although some scholars tend to recognize a strictly Jewish tradition here, which is by no means negligible in historical terms,[18] the whole passage seems more a re-reading of echoes of contacts with Christians over the trial and execution of Jesus. The trial, which according to the Gospels was a hasty affair, is here presented in a better light.[19] The accusation of sorcery twists the tradition of miracles, reformulating calumnies already reported in the Gospels[20] (Matt.12.24–27 par.). The 'leading astray' of Israel, doubtless inspired by Deut.13.2–12,[21] describes the experience of a heretical movement issuing from within it. Though threatened with stoning, a Jewish punishment, Jesus is nevertheless hanged. We could understand this in terms of the Jewish regulations which require the victim, once he has been put to death by stoning, to be hung on a post and exposed to public view until the evening (Deut.21.22-23). However, when applied to Jesus, the verb 'hang' is unequivocal and, as Paul moreover confirms (Gal.3.13), quoting Deut.21.23, it is a periphrasis to denote crucifixion.[22] Blinzler offers a shrewd analysis: 'Apparently the Talmudic tradition represents an effort to reconcile the historical reality somehow or other with the fiction of a purely Jewish trial. As a seducer of the people, Jesus would have had to be been stoned by the Jews, but his death on the Roman cross was too well known to allow of denial. Hence, Jewish tradition speaks of hanging as the Jewish mode of punishment which without of course being a real death penalty bore the closest resemblance to capital punishment.'[23] By fixing the punishment on 'the eve of Passover' or according to a variant, 'the eve of the sabbath and the eve of the Passover', the Talmud follows the Johannine chronology of the passion; it will have been communicated to the Jew who is behind this note. So there is nothing here that we could claim to represent some tradition independent of the Gospels and the Christian version of the facts. In attributing responsibility for the death of Jesus to the Jews alone, this text proves that the person who produced it had no access whatever to the Gospels, but that his knowledge derived simply from Christians who, simplifying to the extreme the tendentious report in the New Testament,[24] accused the Jews of having killed Jesus.

We must attribute the few contacts between the *Toledot Yeshû* and the Gospels to the same type of information. Apart from Voltaire,[25] hardly any educated person has taken seriously these fantastic legends, which came into being during the high Middle Ages, in connection with the story of Jesus. In particular the *Toledot Yeshû* do not provide any scientific confirmation of Jewish responsibility for the trial nor do they illuminate the course it took.[26] The importance of the *Toledot Yeshû* lies elsewhere, and the judgment of Samuel Krauss is still valuable here. According to him, 'each text of the *Toledot Yeshû* is a mirror of the period, which reflects the feelings, aspirations and opinions of a certain part at least of Judaism or of certain Jewish circles'. He goes on: 'This little book can teach us the opinion that the Jews formed of Christianity. That means that its value is not objective, but subjective.'[27]

Christian sources

Outside the Gospels, the Acts of the Apostles and the Pauline corpus, the New Testament is astonishingly discreet about the crucifixion of Jesus[28] – and it is silent about the trial which led to it. Paul makes this punishment a central theme of his theology (I Cor.2.2), without toning it down at all. As for those responsible for the affair, I Timothy (6.13) recalls the 'good confession' which Jesus made to the tribunal of Pontius Pilate,[29] mentioning only the Roman trial, the only one which could inspire faithfulness in Christians who were themselves exposed to the judgment of the imperial authorities at the end of the first century when this Pseudo-Pauline work was written. Without depending visibly on the Gospels, this passage agrees with them in reproducing the same tradition. Before that we have the authentic letters of Paul. Here several scholars hesitate to attribute to him the passage in I Thessalonians (2.13–16) in which, among other condemnations of the Jews, they are said to 'have killed the Lord Jesus'.[30] But this extreme simplification of events is echoed where Paul's pen is indubitably involved. For despite the persistence of exegesis to the contrary, the 'archons' or 'princes of this world' to whom Paul imputes the crucifixion of Christ (I Cor.2.6,8) are not demonic powers but human beings, and this time more probably the Jewish authorities, whose all too human 'wisdom' appears again in the divisions in Corinth.[31] However, so far our harvest has been meagre, and to discover the way in which the trial of Jesus unfolded, we must resort to the four canonical Gospels, with the Acts of the Apostles as an appendix.

Here I shall exclude the contribution of the Christian apocrypha, in this case the Gospel of Peter and the Acts of Pilate or Gospel of Nicodemus. The former (an Akhmimic manuscript discovered in the winter of 1886/7), which has been mutilated, does not add anything to what we can already read in the canonical Gospels, the facts of which it uses. Moreover, it takes us away from these very facts by reason of the ignorance of Palestinian matters which it displays and the contradictions which are shown up by archaeology. We note that the author has pressed the Jewish responsibility for the affair to the maximum: here (3–5) it is Herod and not Pilate who gives the order for Jesus to be led away to execution. As for the Acts of Pilate, we can echo the verdict of G.W.H.Lampe: 'The Acts [of Pilate] draw most of their material from the canonical Gospels, using them eclectically, but depending . . . mainly on the Fourth Gospel for the interrogation of Jesus by Pilate and taking the narrative of the crucifixion from Luke. The non-canonical material, which predominates in the first chapter and in the long section which deals with the resurrection, and is interspersed through the rest of the work alongside material derived from the Gospels, has often been very awkwardly harmonized with the latter and sometimes involves contradictions.'[32] The work does not offer any facts which either illuminate or complement the historical information offered by the canonical Gospels about the trial of Jesus.

The Gospels and the Acts of the Apostles depend at least on a tradition, if not a narrative,[33] which already gave pride of place to the passion of Jesus and recalled its essential course. This fact is remarkable, since it contrasts with the poverty of our information about the earlier activity of Jesus; here it is very difficult to establish any sequence of events, whereas his last hours are the object of a detailed account. If the memory of Christians attached itself to the circumstances of this trial and the capital punishment in which it resulted, that can only be because of the unique importance of this death in the order of faith.[34] The New Testament shows that the object of Christian preaching and the response that it produced was what Paul described with reference to the tradition as: 'that Christ died for our sins in accordance with the scriptures, that he was buried, that he was raised on the third day in accordance with the scriptures' (I Cor.15.3b-4).[35] Paul doubtless thought it useful to relate the passion. But the moment a biographical interest in Jesus is shown, it is natural for attention to be directed towards the essential object of faith. However, this object, because of the horror and 'scandal' inspired by such a death, needed some justification. That is why – as Paul's testimony confirms – these events were recalled only in connection with a reference to the Old Testament, which was thought to describe the features of the suffering Messiah and legitimate him in advance.

That is how a narrative tradition about the passion of Jesus came into being, a tradition which did not keep to the brute facts. As Xavier Léon-Dufour writes,[36] 'the facts were related by believers with a view to communicating, giving birth to and confirming faith. The fundamental event is the event of Easter, a fact which gives a new dimension to the story and which makes it possible to recall the scandalous events which preceded it without toning them down.'

To serve this end, various courses were adopted: a harmonization with the Old Testament texts, which were thought to announce the fate of the suffering Christ; dogmatic themes focussing attention on the divinity of Jesus, his sovereign power, his role in the plan of salvation and, as a consequence, modelling the presentation of facts and giving rise to revelatory sayings; on occasion pointed polemic against the Jews as being those primarily responsible for the death of Jesus, whereas the Romans became secondary; finally, above all in the Gospel of Luke, edifying suggestions for an exemplary portrait of Jesus to be offered to Christians.

What I have just emphasized in fact defines the work of the evangelists. For far from being mere reporters, they put their own stamp on the tradition which they received and the written sources which they used. Each to a different degree made what he received his own work, dealing with it and mixing it in according to one or more perspectives relating to Christian theology or practice. In other words, when we approach these works to derive historical information for them, we must have sufficient idea of the way in which their authors composed them, their aims and the 'tendencies' which might modify, and indeed create, a particular detail or a particular saying.

In addition to this obligation the scholar has another, that of defining as far as possible the relationship between the Gospels. Which of them depends on one or more other Gospels, as a whole or in part, a fact that relativizes the autonomy of its information? Which is witness to an original tradition? If we had evidence of the latter, it would be necessary to compare this tradition with its parallels, not to say its rivals. In the event, the oblique light shed by history generally and by the Jewish and Roman institutions is an indispensable help. The typical example here is the inevitable choice that has to be made between the Johannine version of the trial, in which there is no session of the Sanhedrin, and the Synoptic Gospels, which describe one. But beyond this point, the essential character of which is clear, other elements in the accounts call for research of this kind.

Unfortunately specialists are far from being unanimous on the question of relations between the Gospels: they confront each other with their opinions as though on a battlefield. Are Matthew and Luke dependent on Mark? Did John use the Synoptic Gospels or at least some of them? Did or did not Luke have a special source for the passion narrative? All these questions are given different answers.

To be brief, and to avoid the trap of the dogmatism with which scholars try to reassure themselves, here are some deliberately 'open' remarks.

First, as far as the passion narratives are concerned, nothing obliges us to accept that Matthew used any other *narrative* than that of Mark: the variants in the former can be explained by his own literary, theological and pastoral interests, not to mention those of the Christian communities by whom the evangelist was influenced and whose heritage he received. It is more difficult to decide in the case of Luke,[37] since a large number of scholars detect the use of a special source for his passion narrative. This is possible, and it is unwise to be definitive on this point. But we need to take account of the following points. First of all, it is not because a particular episode does not appear in the other Gospels (for example, the appearance of Jesus before Herod Antipas) that scholars are led to suspect the use of a continuous source: the incorporation of erratic facts from the tradition could be enough to account for this phenomenon.[38] Secondly, such a difference or addition in the presentation of the facts can be explained if we pay attention to the parenetic or christological imperatives of the author throughout his redaction: we might think of the account of the agony, or the words of Jesus on the cross which are clearly meant to be an example; and did a source lead Luke to suppress the scourging as such and Jesus' cry of abandonment? Moreover, Luke is a professional narrator, so that he was well able to create variants which he thought profitable for his readers, if only to fill a gap and obtain a better literary balance (for example by editing the accusation by the members of the Sanhedrin before Pilate in

23.2). Finally, it is important to note that the order of the episodes of the passion in Luke is generally the same as in Mark. Of the twenty episodes counted by Fitzmyer in Luke, eighteen appear in Mark in almost the same order, so that the overall framework is identical in both cases.[39] Thus we are not obliged to give the passion narrative priority: here Luke could well have used Mark freely, as he does in the rest of his Gospel.

The question of the relationship between the Fourth Gospel and the three others is even more tricky.[40] Did John use them directly, as a whole or in part? Or is he dependent on one or more traditions or sources to which the Synoptic evangelists equally had access? The problem becomes more complicated if we remember that John was not written all at once and that recourse to the Synoptic Gospels at the final stage of its composition does not imply the same dependence on them as in the earlier strata. Particularly in the case of the passion narrative, some scholars attach importance to Bultmann's theory of the existence of a 'passion source' used by John, which will have had few contacts with the Synoptics, even if they modify it somewhat. It is sometimes suggested that other sources or traditions equally known to the Synoptics will have been added to this source. The matter is too complicated to be settled here in a peremptory way. Let us just say first that to deny any contact between John and the Synoptics is to close one's eyes to the evidence, but that this is no longer the case if one says that this contact presupposes a direct relationship: we can in fact ask whether such dependence is not rather to be put at the level of the sources. However, the fact that we find in John, outside the passion narrative, elements belonging to the Markan passion narrative (thus for the 'agony' in Mark 14.34 compare John 12.27; or see the charge of 'blasphemy' in John 10.33–36, which evokes Mark 14.61–64) or in Luke (compare John 10.24–25; Luke 22.67–68; John 19.12 and Luke 23.20–21) gives, rather, the impression of a free use by John of his predecessors to fill out his own composition. As for the actual passion narrative, the Johannine version offers several points of contact, some of them verbal, with the same account in Matthew and Luke;[41] this phenomenon is difficult to explain without a direct influence.

There is less basis for saying that John had a document at his disposal giving a continuous account of Jesus' passion. On the other hand it is certain that he hands on to us some new traditions, a number of which are of real historical interest. The nocturnal appearance before Annas is one of the most valuable. Nor did John invent the names *Lithostroton* and *Gabbatha*.[42] But in several episodes, the features which distinguish this Gospel from the others bear the stamp of its author, in both form and contact, to such an extent that one can see no need to envisage documentation other than the Synoptic Gospels (e.g. in comparing the parallel sessions before Pilate).

As a provisional conclusion, which is nevertheless one that is highly probable, we may say:

– it is almost impossible to establish the existence of a continuous source underlying the Johannine account of the passion;

– unless we accept that the only possible use of an earlier Gospel is that to which Matthew and Luke bear witness, we cannot brush aside the idea that John knew the Synoptic Gospels and was influenced by them;

– John collected traditions independent of the Synoptics;

– in the passion narrative John shows the same independent personality as in the rest of his Gospel, and his involvement in the redaction is considerable, both in reporting the facts and in the sayings.

The Gospels are of unequal value for historical enquiry. In the event, Matthew and Luke add hardly anything to what we already find in Mark. Nothing that they add to him, and none of the differences between him and them, even if these additions or differences cannot systematically be attributed to the creation of the two evangelists, offers any guarantee that allows us to recognize the real facts here.[43] So we have to examine Mark and John for traces of their origins.

I have already made the essential points about the possibilities offered by John, and each episode of the trial will give us an occasion to assess his contribution. There remains Mark. Here we would love to know his background, i.e. the written or oral material which he had at his disposal. Unfortunately, discussion of the sources of Mark, especially in the passion narrative, is far from closed.[44] Do we have to think of an already-formed block, first handed down orally and used in the communities, while recognizing that other elements have been inserted into it? Or were there only independent pieces before Mark?[45] There have also been other suggestions, for example that there was a 'long narrative' issuing largely in the Gospel of Mark, or a 'short narrative' comprising crucifixion, burial and Easter message, according to the scheme of preaching preserved in I Cor.15.3–4, along with yet other more adventurous theories.[46] At certain points the text of this Gospel shows seams which allow us to presuppose the existence of something earlier which will have been worked on subsequently. However, there is insufficient evidence to allow us to state that Mark had a consecutive narrative of the passion.

Whatever this narrative may have been, if it existed at all, and even if one can discover its main outlines, the historian is not excused from submitting it to a critical examination. Nor, *a priori*, would it be any more untouched by amplifications and adaptations than the Gospel which used it.[47] One may just as well keep to Mark as a witness to the tradition of the trial and execution of Jesus, using the Fourth Gospel as essential documentation from the Christian side. In the last analysis, everything stems from the first communities of Palestine, and that of Jerusalem in particular, certain of whose members could have spoken about what happened at Gethsemane and on Golgotha, having been informed by direct or indirect witnesses (here one thinks of Simon of Cyrene).[48] Once piously received, the memories of these facts were handed down in the churches, never as brute facts but, as I have said, always wrapped in an interpretative reading to which the evangelists put the last touches.

2

The Arrest

In the four Gospels, the first episode of the passion proper relates the arrest of Jesus. Mark (14.43–52) offers us a considerable historical basis to which the other Gospels add nothing essential.

The place

The scene is set in 'a place which was called Gethsemane' (Mark 14.32), to which Jesus had withdrawn with his disciples. The term *kêpos*, 'garden', in John 18.1, which corresponds to the Markan word *chôrion* ('ground', 'domain'),[1] is more precise. Also according to John, this garden was 'beyond the brook Kidron', information without the least religious relevance which there is no problem in retaining. The name 'Gethsemane' renders the Hebrew–Aramaic *gat shemanî(m)(n)*,[2] 'oil press'. Luke (22.39) did not think that his readers would be interested in knowing this local name; he only gives them the name 'Golgotha' (Luke 23.33; cf. Mark 15.22). Here he is content with the general indication of place which he is given in Mark 14.26, where we learn that the group went towards the 'Mount of Olives'.

Luke (22.39) also shows us Jesus going to this place 'as was his custom'. Here the evangelist is referring to what he has written earlier (21.37) about Jesus' behaviour in Jerusalem: during the day he taught in the temple, and he spent the night on the Mount of Olives, doubtless to pray there.[3] These notes are steeped in Lukan expressions and themes, and so have no great historical value. According to John 18.2, 'Jesus often stayed[4] there with his disciples', information which is as trivial as it is useful, with no other origin than the apparent need to justify Judas' knowledge of the place where Jesus was.

From all the facts on which the Gospels agree we can accept that Jesus was arrested in a place, doubtless a garden, called *Gat shemanî*, beyond the Kidron, either at the foot of or on the lower slopes of the Mount of Olives.

By whom and in whose name was Jesus arrested?

Mark (14.43) describes the squad charged with arresting Jesus as a 'band with swords and clubs', i.e. an armed troop,[5] and this is what John summarily calls it (18.3: *hopla*). John adds 'lanterns' and 'torches', a detail which is understandable, given the hour. What is more difficult to square with reality, at least for some scholars, is the bearing of arms on the eve of the Passover, given that the Passover had the character of a sabbath.[6] But if we accept that the Markan chronology of the passion is the right one,[7] it is improbable that the Jewish authorities thought it illegal for the henchmen serving in the squad to be equipped to deal with active resistance: here the already ancient rule (I Macc.2.39–41) that one could defend oneself on any day of the week where there was mortal danger applied.[8]

The squad is said to have been sent by 'the high priests, the scribes and the elders' (Mark 14.33). This triple enumeration, from which we can recognize the composition of the Sanhedrin, indicates that this police operation was completely official on the Jewish side. Mark indicates this three more times (8.31; 14.53; 15.1), and we cannot doubt that where he abbreviates the list,[9] he is following the same plan, everywhere with the intention of attributing responsibility for the death of Jesus to the supreme authority of Judaism. However, since the high priest or high priests are always mentioned in the preparation and execution of this murderous enterprise, and sometimes only them, we can attach much more weight to them than to the other Jewish parties and count their involvement among the facts handed down by the tradition.

Are those ordered to make the arrest the Levites responsible for maintaining order and security within the temple? In fact we know of no operation of this kind being entrusted to Levites outside the sanctuary.[10] John (18.2) speaks of 'servants [*hypêretai*] of the chief priests and Pharisees'. The Pharisees are an addition which has no historical value. As for the 'servants',[11] they recall more the lay minions at the disposition of the courts, whom Abba Joseph ben Hanin doubtless remembered when composing this ballad which has been preserved in the Tosefta and the Talmud,[12] and which refers to the priestly families at the time of the Second Temple:

> Woe unto me because of the house of Baithos [Boethus];
>   woe unto me for their lances !
> Woe unto me because of the house of Hanin,
>   woe unto me for their whisperings!
> Woe unto me because of the house of Qathros
>   woe unto me because of their reed pens![13]
> Woe unto me because of the house of Ishmael b.Phiabi,
>   woe unto me because of their fists!
> For they are high priests and their sons are treasurers
>   and their sons-in-law are Temple overseers
> *And their servants smite the people with sticks.*[14]

In addition to the Jewish militia, the Fourth Gospel involves the 'cohort' (*speira*), with the 'tribune' or 'chiliarch' in command (John 18.3, 12). Beyond question this is part of the Roman garrison stationed in the fortress Antonia in Jerusalem.[15] It is improbable that this troop of 600 men took part in the arrest of Jesus, not because the numbers would have been manifestly excessive in the circumstances (after all, John could have been thinking of only a detachment of the cohort), but because that goes against subsequent events. In fact it is hard to see the Roman soldiers, under the command of their leader, taking Jesus to the high priest, which according to the unanimous testimony of the Gospels is what happened. Furthermore, during the trial Pilate seems to ignore this intervention entirely, and according to all the witnesses those who took Jesus to him were only Jews. If we add the total silence of the Synoptic Gospels, we can regard this contribution by the Roman army as a fiction, whatever its origin and the use of it made by the evangelist.

The role of Judas

The four accounts agree on the role of Judas as the guide to those who arrested Jesus. According to the Gospels, this action is not his only one in the tragedy which led Jesus to Calvary. Earlier we see Judas offering his services to the high priests to deliver Jesus to them and them promising him money.[16]

This mediation is facilitated by the fact that Judas Iscariot belongs to the group of Jesus' disciples; moreover he is described in the Gospels as 'one of the Twelve' (Mark 14.10,43 par.). But is this a historical fact?[17]

The presence of Jesus among the Twelve is denied, first, by scholars who refuse to accept that the group was formed by Jesus himself. But it is easier to accept that it originated before Easter than to suppose that it was a creation by the first community. Certainly the Twelve had their place in that community at the beginning, as Paul attests (I Cor.15.5). However, this is in a piece of the tradition which he inherited, and he himself shows no personal knowledge of the group. During his first visit to Jerusalem, at least three years after his conversion, he did not meet this group, nor does he give any indication of its presence or its direction in the community (Gal.1.19). If we want to put its origin within the community, we end up saying that the group ceased to exist very soon after it had been formed. It is more probable that it was founded by Jesus and re-formed after the flight, which we shall be discussing later. It was then that it was rewarded by a vision of the Risen Christ, as Paul attests in I Cor.15.5.[18]

Now in the three lists of the Twelve in the Gospels we find the name of Judas in last place. Though there was a concern to suppress him, people felt obliged to mention him and found it difficult to substitute another name for him. No such name could in fact be found.[19]

Finally, although scholars have wanted to see the manifest disloyalty of Judas as a warning to Christians tempted to apostatize, such a degree of inventiveness goes beyond the liberties which the evangelists (or their sources) allow themselves in the realm of facts.

So we must leave Judas his place in the college of Twelve and his role in the tragic end of Jesus.

However, it is important here to define this role. One constant in the Gospels is that Judas was the one who 'delivered up' Jesus. However, the expression is a vague one: moreover it belongs in a context where Judas is not the only one involved, that of the whole judicial action against Jesus at the end of which he was to be put to death – and by derivation the judicial action which would be taken against his disciples.[20] Can we be more precise about the role of Judas by utilizing the scene of his intervention with the high priest as described in Mark 14.10–11? Certainly its matter-of-factness offers good historical guarantees, though we do not know what could have been said in the circumstances.[21] The pejorative reading of Matthew (26.14–16), according to which Judas was engaged in a sordid trade, is little help here. The man's greediness is certainly indicated by John (12.4–6), but we cannot affirm that this is not a feature imagined in order to blacken his person. Moreover John, unlike Matthew, does not introduce this taint in describing Judas's action against his master. In reality one can only guess at the motives which guided him in his defection.[22]

It is perfectly plausible that these led him to Gethsemane to guide the guards ordered to arrest Jesus there, and the Fourth Gospel takes this line when it explains that Judas 'knew the place' (John 18.2). We can understand how Jesus, feeling threatened, should have withdrawn outside the city, and how only someone who knew him would have known where to find him.

Jesus also had to be identified. It is not in fact certain that his notoriety was as great as John tells us (12.11,19) and that any militia leader would have recognized him at first sight. We might add that the groves of Gethsemane, even when lit by torches (John 18.3), were hardly like a major street by night. Mark (14.44), followed by Matthew (26.48), tells us of a 'sign' agreed by Judas and the troop: 'the one to whom I shall give a kiss is he'.

This mark of respect and veneration,[23] normal on the part of a disciple in ordinary circumstances, is less so in the case of an arrest by the police; here a gesture of the hand to identify Jesus in the semi-darkness would have been enough. The hatefulness of the action is here taken to its limit, and the Bible, through similar examples,[24] would have been enough to inspire this detail.

Nor is it in keeping with the situation to hear Judas telling the band, 'Seize him and lead him away safely!'[25] (Mark 14.44), as if he was the leader instead of merely the one who was pointing Jesus out. What are we to think of a command which, in the present instance, borders on the ridiculous? The police knew better than anyone what they had to do.

We may conclude that the aim of the narrative, which is moral and intended as a deterrent, resulted in increasing the responsibility and the role of Judas in the arrest of Jesus. Judas shows himself right at the head of Mark's account; the band is 'with him' and he gives it orders. Jesus' intimate friend hands over his master with a kiss. Everything is done to bring him to the fore and, through him, to warn Christians of what they will be tempted to do as apostates. In fact, while Judas is not to be excluded from the operation, his role must have been subordinate and momentary. Moreover he then disappears from the scene of the passion for ever.

A brawl at Gethsemane?

A very brief mention of the arrest (Mark 14.46) shows the evangelist's veneration for the victim of this action (the same is true of the scourging and the crucifixion). But the narrative does not stop there, and immediately passes on to the transfer of Jesus to the Jewish authorities. An incident takes place after Jesus has been apprehended. Mark writes: 'But one of those who stood by drew his sword, and struck the slave of the high priest and cut off his ear'[26] (14.47).

There is no commentary at all on this. Both its position in the narrative (Jesus has already been arrested) and the laconic way in which it is narrated are surprising. Who are these people from whom the aggressor comes? Many scholars leave Mark and draw their inspiration from the other Gospels. Matthew (26.51) and Luke (22.49–50) attribute the gesture to a disciple, and in both cases this is a defensive act on behalf of Jesus. The same is true in John (18.10), who makes the action more specific by naming Simon Peter as the one who uses his sword. According to a number of exegetes or historians, Mark by his vague formula is prudently covering up what the other evangelists disclose:[27] Jesus was in fact accompanied by armed disciples ready to intervene in case of attack, who did not hesitate to pass over to action. If that is the case, we have to allow that Matthew, Luke and John derived their precision from elsewhere than Mark, in a tradition which was more faithful to reality.

But is not the importance of the scene exaggerated? It already becomes less prominent if, instead of seeing 'those standing there' as the disciples, we see them as the police. At all events this is the perspective of Mark, for whom this expression never denotes the disciples[28] and who in this passage sees to it that can be no misunderstanding here: those whom Jesus reproaches for their armed intervention (14.48) are those in whose ranks the aggressor is. So he is someone in the squad.

Sometimes it is supposed that an accident took place in the darkness, an involuntary clumsiness for which the high priest's servant paid the price. But when is this scuffle to be put? The text of Mark gives the impression that it is an appendix added to a story which has already been concluded since Jesus has been arrested, while what follows (14.48–49) is even more clearly additional. If on the other hand we know that to have one's ear cut off meant shame and ridicule for people of antiquity, and that among the Jews a mutilated person could not take part in the cult, we have no difficulty in seeing in this incident a feature by which the narrator, not without some malice, avenges the insult inflicted on Jesus by indirectly involving the high priest, the person mainly responsible for the arrest and its sequel.[29]

In attributing the intervention to a disciple, the other versions of the incident give Jesus an opportunity to speak to Christian readers and, in Luke (22.51), to give them a good example of forgiving offences and of love of enemy in the healing of the wounded ear. The historicity of the basic event remains doubtful, despite the more precise details given by the Fourth Evangelist: the fact that he gives names to those involved in this little drama – the aggressor is Peter and his victim is a certain Malchus – is not a criteria to which one could appeal without reservations. The name 'Simon Peter' appears in the New Testament above all in John and, although this is not an absolute rule, it can be said that 'storytellers do delight in individualizing their characters by supplying them with names'.[30] Similarly, the name of the wounded man, whose kinsman we shall meet later in the high priest's palace (John 18.26), could well derive from narrative conventions, like this last detail.[31]

The flight of the disciples

The words of Jesus, which according to Mark 14.48–49 par. are addressed to the guards, take no account of the incident of the sword blow and develop a defence which relates to a context earlier in the Gospel, the presence of Jesus in the temple – a purely literary framework in Mark 12.27–13.2. So these words betray their origin at the same time as they indicate those to whom they are addressed: the readers of the Gospel.

On the other hand, Mark has not created the note about the general flight of the disciples (14.50), reproduced by Matthew (26.56b), out of nothing. Matthew in fact removes any trace of doubt by his explicit mention of 'the disciples'. Mark does not do this, perhaps moved by the same feeling of embarrassment which has led Luke to suppress this unedifying feature completely. However, the Markan context allows no hesitation about the identity of the fugitives: apart from the guards, the only ones who can escape are those around Jesus. Badly placed in the text, this disbanding naturally follows the arrest (Mark 14.46), which it extends with the same economy of words. The prophetic announcement of it in Mark 14.27 (citing Zech.13.7) does not rob it in any way of its reality, nor is it contradicted by the presence of Peter in the high priest's palace.[32] The fact of the disciples' flight is of historical importance, because it makes it possible to exclude any trace of a conspiracy from Jesus' plans: confederates would also have been arrested. Now we can see them disappearing freely into the night. The hierarchs restrict themselves to neutralizing the one who inspired the movement, certain that a handful of Galileans will not be able to stand the loss of their master.

The next note, peculiar to Mark 14.51–52, is less laconic. We can understand how the other evangelists will have regarded as frivolous this sudden appearance of a young man, hastily dressed, who, when seized by one of the police, struggles free and takes flight, leaving behind the linen cloth which enveloped him. This almost grotesque incident, which is fertile ground for the most adventurous speculations, does not in fact cloak any secret. Indubitably a historical reminiscence, it is used by Mark to complete the picture of the débacle which has already been presented: this unknown young man 'followed' Jesus with the other disciples and, like them, he 'fled', leaving Jesus irrevocably in the hands of his enemies.[33]

3

Why was Jesus Arrested?

The question which forms the title of this chapter is one of the most formidable faced by the exegete and historian. That is all the more the case since it goes beyond the simple and immediate cause of the arrest to extend to all the activity and the words of Jesus. We are led to ask: what mission did Jesus attribute to himself which led him to adopt positions and hold views which led him to Calvary? We know that research into the historical Jesus is still open and that all the efforts in this sphere have failed to lead to unanimous conclusions, given the state of the documentation. Nor will the reader be surprised to find in this chapter certain reservations, and proposals which are to a large extent hypothetical.

However, one point may be regarded as certain: as we have just seen, the arrest of Jesus was a purely Jewish affair. Mark emphasizes the official character of the operation and attributes responsibility for it to the three groups which made up the Sanhedrin. But we have already been able to note that in his account of the passion the same evangelist brings out the general and predominant role of the 'high priests'. We must now return to this aspect, in order to be more precise and to draw conclusions about the reasons for such an act.

Who were the high priests?

In the New Testament and in Josephus the word *archiereus* is used both in the singular and in the plural to denote the person of the high priest and a group of persons belonging to the higher degrees of the Jewish priesthood respectively. In English versions the same word is sometimes translated 'chief priests', which confuses matters somewhat. Whereas in the former case the function is well defined, that cannot be said of the latter. Here there are two competing explanations. One, which goes back to the eminent historian Emil Schürer,[1] regards the *archiereis* as a body composed of the high priest in office, the high priests who had been deposed (as they frequently were at that time) and members of the priestly aristocracy from among whom the high priest was chosen. According to the other theory, put forward by Joachim Jeremias,[2] the *archiereis* formed a 'college' which exercised authority over the cult and external order of the temple; while they came from priestly families, they were not identified with these.

Jeremias's criticisms of the rival theory are developed from three pieces of evidence. The first is that of Josephus,[3] in whose writing the term in question can apply only to two retired high priests, and does not include their close relations. The second piece of evidence is that of the Acts of the Apostles (4.6), which lists in connection with the appearance of Peter and John before the Sanhedrin, 'Annas the high priest and Caiaphas and John [or Jonathan] and Alexander and all who were of the high-priestly family' [*ek genous arch-ieratikou*].[3] Now, Jeremias notes, it is inconceivable that all the men from high-priestly families could have sat in a council limited to seventy-one members. Finally the Mishnah,[4] which mentions the 'sons of the high priests' (*benê kohanîm gedolîm*) who exercised juridical functions, is not denoting the children of the high priests but, in keeping with the traditional Hebrew expression, a body which they formed, 'a tribunal taking decisions in matters of civil law relating to the priests'.

However, none of these arguments clinches the matter, as moreover Jeremias recognizes in the case of some of them, and the existence of the 'college' in question cannot be regarded as historically proven. The objection that not all the members of priestly families could have been part of the Sanhedrin would be decisive in itself if this were the meaning of the phrase in Acts 4.6. But on the one hand, we cannot claim that Luke's expressions are completely rigorous: the emphasis is in place here, and Luke is a fanatic for totality, not to mention the inaccuracy which makes Annas actually exercise the office of high priest. On the other hand, when we know that nepotism was rampant in priestly circles,[5] we can understand how the highest functions in the administration of the sanctuary would have been entrusted to members of these families, who by this route would have had access to the Sanhedrin.

The people mentioned above would not have been the sole members of the Sanhedrin, which was presided over by the high priest. In the time of Jesus and the apostles, if we follow the New Testament and Josephus,[6] there were also 'scribes' (*grammateis*), professional lawyers, the majority of whom were Pharisees, and the lay nobility (the 'elders'), who, with the priests, attached themselves above all to the Sadducean movement. While we must recognize that the influence of the Pharisees, which was considerable on the population, may well have had repercussions on the Sanhedrin,[7] the fact remains that the priestly element held the reins of power there along the lines of the post-exilic hierocracy. In fact, in the lists in the New Testament where we recognize the Sanhedrin, the high priests are always at the head, an order confirmed by Josephus.[8] However, their power was not exercised only within the framework of the supreme council of the nation. The high priest and the hierarchs who surrounded him could engage in police operations without needing to call an assembly of the Sanhedrin. Specifically, these police operations were under the 'captain of the temple', the senior official after the high priest.[9]

It was on the order of this last that Jesus was apprehended. That confirms the facts in the Gospels about the key role of the 'high priests' from this beginning, as throughout the trial which follows. In this case we have to suppose that Jesus was charged with having managed to displease the masters of the temple and the chief leaders of the nation in particular.

This generalization is easy to deduce. It is much more difficult to say why Jesus drew down on himself the hostility of these circles. A first approach suggests itself to anyone seeking to answer this question, namely to investigate one or more events which could have prompted an intervention.

The entry with the palms

Among the events which precede the passion in the Gospels, the entry of Jesus into Jerusalem, if it took place as we are told, could not have left the priestly authorities indifferent. A truly messianic demonstration in which an exultant crowd escorted Jesus and celebrated in him the restoration of the Davidic kingdom which was so long awaited (Mark 11.9–10), the 'entry with the palms', would have attracted the attention and prompted the fear of the high priest and his entourage, whose role 'as collaborators' will be emphasized later: the anti-Roman political impact of the ovation given to Jesus was in this case all too visible. But why wait? Why not nip in the bud an act which could only be seen as a restoration of the monarchy by popular acclamation? Even if the local authorities had been reluctant to intervene on the spot, preferring more discreet action and resorting to a stratagem, as the Gospels report (Mark 14.1–2), one doubts whether the Romans would have allowed a demonstration of this kind, to all appearances directed against them, to be staged under their noses and so to speak before their very eyes. In the situation in Jerusalem at that time, tolerance on their part is unthinkable: Jesus would have been arrested and the soldiers would have gone on to pick up his disciples.

So we can remove from the historical reasons for the arrest of Jesus the entry into Jerusalem as described by the Gospels. Do we have to think of a more limited move which, despite everything, could have aroused suspicions in the minds of the authorities, suspicions which later prompted an arrest in order to be on the safe side? Many hypotheses are possible as to what facts were the seed for a narrative of a conventional kind, steeped in messianic faith and fed by the Old Testament.[10] However, there is nothing that obliges us to accept that these facts had any connection with the drama which began in Gethsemane, or that the incident was included in the brief for the trial ordered by Pilate, since the documents are silent here. On the other hand, other suggestions come to mind when we consider the sequence of events related in the Gospels.[11] They do not strictly relate to politics, nor are they connected with the Roman empire. Could not Jesus have provoked the high priests by his attitude towards the temple?

The incident in the temple

The four Gospels[12] report a scene in which we see Jesus engage in a spectacular action against the market in the temple. According to the Gospel of John, the event took place at the beginning of Jesus' public life; the Synoptic Gospels put it at the end. It is not possible to come to a firm conclusion about the chronology. Mark's schematism, followed by the two other Synoptics, which reduces Jesus' journeys to Jerusalem to one, offers us fewer historical guarantees than the Fourth Gospel[13] when it reports that Jesus made three pilgrimages to the Holy City before the last, which put an end to his career. But John is less certain when he sets the incident at the temple during the first of these visits: at this point there is every chance that the episode, arranged and composed as the negative counterpart to the 'wedding at Cana',[14] relates above all to the evangelist's literary and theological plan.

The objection is often made to John's chronology that if Jesus had acted in this way at the beginning of his ministry, he would have definitively compromised it by laying himself open to the revenge of the Jewish authorities. Other scholars go even further and bluntly contest the very historicity of the fact, emphasizing that such a demonstration would immediately have prompted a reaction from the temple police, not to mention the Roman garrison in the Antonia, a fortress situated at the north-east corner of the temple forecourt, from which the soldiers could go down a staircase to intervene immediately in case of trouble.

In reality, no matter at what point in the life of Jesus the event is to be put, its basic historicity is certain. Without precedent or biblical model, it has unique features and could not have been invented. However, we cannot accept it without limiting its scope.

The temple market occupied part of the Court of the Gentiles, a vast area of around 450 by 300 metres.[15] Merchants and money-changers could not have been driven out from there by one man, however robust, not even if he were armed with a whip as in the dramatic scene in the Gospel of John. The scene depicted by C.H.Dodd, who envisages that this expulsion took place 'with a minimum of disorder' and solely under the moral pressure of

Jesus, indeed with the agreement of a large number of people, is better suited to the lounge of an old people's home than an eastern market place.[16] The theory of a military-type operation with the collaboration of armed disciples is far more natural in such a setting,[17] but historically that is even more improbable than the previous hypothesis. Martin Hengel has tersely rejected it, showing that given the surveillance of the place by Roman troops – particularly at festival times – 'any tumult of any dimension would immediately have brought the garrison on the scene, above all since Pilate was not squeamish on this point'.[18]

On the other hand, one can accept that Jesus performed a prophetic action by overturning a few stalls and banking counters. Limited in scope, and done in the crowd, this action to which the disciples were witnesses and which they remembered could have passed relatively unnoticed.

But what significance did Jesus attach to it? It is supposed that he accompanied his gesture with comments after the manner of the prophets of old. There is little chance that the words which the evangelists put on his lips here go back to him,[19] since of the two antithetical quotations of Isa.56.7 and Jer.7.11, one reproduces the Greek text of the Septuagint almost word for word and the other is based on it. It all comes from a Christian pen which fiercely condemns the trade practised in the area of the sanctuary, announcing, in the form of a punishment, that it will be suppressed in favour of a universal cult.[20] If we remove this saying on the grounds that it cannot possible indicate Jesus' intentions here, it is not easy to discover what these intentions were. Critics today offer three interpretations of the gesture. The first and most common sees it as being the symbol of a purification of temple worship. According to the second, Jesus will have wanted to signify the extension of the worship of the true God to all the peoples called to the kingdom. Finally, it is thought that Jesus was illustrating the destruction of the temple in advance. The first and the second interpretation are influenced by the commentary of the evangelists on Jesus. The third firmly excludes this.

The second interpretation, which exploits the fact that the incident takes place in the Court of the *Gentiles*, is easy to refute:

'we recall that the Son of David was popularly expected to "cleanse Jerusalem of the Gentiles". Jesus wanted it cleansed *for* the Gentiles', writes C.H.Dodd.[21] But no matter what may have been the position of Jesus over non-Jews and his interest in them, too much is attached here to the location of the event, given that the forecourt in question, though Gentiles indeed had access to it, was more full of Jews, above all at the time of the Passover, as the Gospels indicate. On the other hand, the place was the best spot for performing a public act that could arouse attention.[22]

The first opinion, which is that of the broad majority, can draw on other cases gleaned from the Gospels: this 'purification' matches other adjustments to Judaism made by Jesus with a view to a return to the authentic will of God.[23] Moreover the Bible and ancient Judaism attest critical attitudes towards the practice of the temple cult. The prophecies of Malachi announce the coming of a divine messenger who 'will purify the sons of Levi and refine them like gold and silver' (3.3). The Psalms of Solomon condemn the Hasmonean priests for being 'led astray from the holy temple of God' in violation of all cultic and moral laws (8.8–13). Similar criticisms are directed against the official clergy by the Essenes of the Dead Sea: the 'Wicked Priest has committed abominations and soiled the sanctuary of God . . . he has stolen the goods of the poor' (1QpH 12.8). Now we know that the temple administration, which was in the hands of the high priests, exercised control over at least some products and that some members of the corporation had shops.[24] It can be added that according to the Tosefta,[25] love of money and mutual hatred provoked the deportation of the Jews after the destruction of the temple. Reinforced by these facts, a large number of scholars see the scene described in the Gospels as the expression of a concern for reform which, far from being opposed to the temple and its worship, militated in its favour, requiring that this worship should be performed in a pure and disinterested way. By forbidding the carrying of any object through the temple (Mark 11.16) in the same context, Jesus would be confirming his concern to increase respect for the sanctuary.

This last order is sometimes interpreted as being aimed at cult objects, and therefore as being opposed to them. However, whatever this ban may be, the argument that here is only a 'purification' of the temple cult comes up against an indubitable truth on which the third interpretation is mainly founded.[26]

This truth is that the temple market, far from resembling the trade in objects of piety which takes place around our sanctuaries, was a necessity in the practice of the cult. For without this market it would have been impossible to pay the temple tax on the spot, since this required money to be changed;[27] nor would it have been possible to acquire animals for sacrifices. The temple tax entailed the annual payment by every male Israelite above the age of thirty of a half-shekel in the month of Adar (February –March).[28] The money paid for this tax had to be the ancient Tyrian coinage formerly used in Palestine by the Jews, which was not legal tender under the Romans. Hence the need to establish money-changers, especially at the edge of the sanctuary, for the convenience of pilgrims. The fact that these functionaries charged a commission (*qolbon*) for their services – though the opinion of the rabbis differed on the destination of these emoluments – does not make their function a swindle at the expense of the population. As for the trade in animals, it was easier for pilgrims to obtain a dove locally to offer as a sacrifice than to bring one down from Galilee or elsewhere, with the risk of damaging it on the way and thus making it unfit for the cult.

So we may conclude that in attacking the market, Jesus was indirectly attacking what this market provided for, nothing less than the sacrificial worship of the temple.[29] It has to be added that Jesus, unlike the critics mentioned above, never utters a word censuring the priests in the performance of their duties.[30] This suggests that he had in mind something more than the actual practice of the cult. As for the gesture itself, the fact that he 'overthrew' (*katastrephein*) the tables and chairs (Mark 11.15 par.) readily evokes destruction, above all if it was inspired by biblical language,[31] whereas other gestures, like pouring out water, better represent the idea of purification.

Mark (11.18) writes that the news of the incident 'came to the ears of the high priests and scribes' and that it prompted them to seek a means of putting Jesus to death. This information is of doubtful historical value and is to be seen more as one of the evangelist's 'refrains', linked with other mentions of this murder plan (Mark 3.6; 12.12; 14.1–2), to prepare the reader for the climax of the passion. This judgment is confirmed by the total absence of any echo of this scene in the sequence of events following the arrest of Jesus. However, interpreted as a symbol of destruction, it accords with the sayings in which Jesus, this time explicitly, announces the destruction of the temple, and which will play a prominent part in his trial. In other words, this gesture, far from being an isolated act of momentary importance, has a place in an overall conception relating to temple worship. That is how it could have played its part in leading to Jesus' arrest.[32]

Sayings against the temple

The interpretation proposed above establishes a connection between Jesus' action in the temple market and the sayings in the Gospel about the destruction of the temple. There are two of these sayings, and their content is not exactly the same.

One appears in the account of the session of the Sanhedrin in which Jesus is judged and condemned. According to the witnesses who appear there, Jesus is said to have declared that he would destroy the sanctuary and rebuilt it (Mark 14.58 par. Matt.26.61). This saying is reflected in the sarcastic comments which Jesus had to endure on Calvary (Mark 15.20–30 par Matt.27.40) and in what is imputed to Stephen in Acts 6.14. The Fourth Evangelist (John 2.19) uses it to compose the extension which he makes to his account of the incident in the temple.

The other saying is the prophecy of Jesus at the head of his great discourse on the end of the world. It announces the total destruction of the sanctuary (Mark 13.2). Another oracle of Jesus can be associated with it, namely the one that he utters in front of Jerusalem according to Luke 19.41–44, where without specifically having the temple in mind, he announces the destruction of the city.[33]

Let us begin with the second saying. In Mark 13.2 it appears wrapped in a short composition of which it was part even before

Mark incorporated the whole passage into his work.[34] The announcement of the destruction of the temple with 'You see these great buildings' cannot have been handed down as an isolated sentence and presupposes a particular context. However, this context has the same character as all the other compositions collected in the Gospels, where the way in which sentences are embedded in such narratives or dialogues betrays a literary origin by its artificial aspect. The sentence itself has been glossed by the evangelist, whose taste for redundant words can be recognized in 'that will not be thrown down' with the verb *katalyein*, which indicates a borrowing from the other tradition included in the trial (Mark 14.58).

An announcement of the destruction of the temple has biblical antecedents and more or less contemporary analogies.[35] But the expression 'stone upon stone' can be found as such only in Haggai 2.15,[36] in a reference to the rebuilding of the temple after the exile. The reference to the temple in Mark 13.2 clashes with the prediction, in the same terms, of the destruction of the *city* in Luke 19.44, within a composition the autonomy of which is sufficiently certain.[37] So a choice has to be made between two traditional versions. Against the choice recently made by Lloyd Gaston, I prefer that of Jacques Schlosser, who writes:[38] 'It seems to me preferable and more convincing to emphasize the rarity of the expression "stone upon stone". As we have seen, this appears only once in the Old Testament, and in this single passage (Hag.2.15) it refers to the temple. Though this observation is not in itself conclusive, it suggests that we should give priority to the reference to the temple and thus to Mark 13.2.'

It does not necessarily follow that this is an authentic saying of Jesus. Without doubt, and Schlosser is right to emphasize the fact,[39] the disappearance of the temple accords with the eschatological horizon of Jesus as we see it according to the Synoptic Gospels. In the perspective of the kingdom of God, when from henceforth harmony has been established between God and his creatures, what need is there for a sacrificial cult which is largely expiatory? It is not improbable that Jesus, borrowing the crude formulae of his predecessors, announced – by choice in Jerusalem and during his last stay in the city - that of this impressive cultic complex, a monument to an era ready to pass away, there would no longer be 'stone upon stone'.

However, this very borrowing and this anthological language (despite its rarity, the expression 'stone upon stone' is part of that) cast doubt on the particular form of the saying in Mark 13.2. And this doubt increases when we note that this same saying competes with the other sayings about the destruction of the temple, the content of which is similar but the interpretation of which is far more difficult. By comparison, the saying which we have just examined looks more like an easier recasting, inspired by the Old Testament.[40]

According to the deposition of the false witnesses in the trial of Jesus and other passages in the Gospels, Jesus will have claimed that he would destroy the temple, or at least rebuild it after its destruction. This last form of the announcement appears after the incident in the temple, in John 2.19: 'Destroy this temple, and in three days I will raise it up.' Whatever may be the dependence of John on Mark and the other Synoptics, everything combines to establish the later character of this version compared with the others: in addition to philological observations,[41] it is clear that the application by John of this saying to the resurrection of Christ has largely coloured it, while reducing its asperity. On the lips of those who mock Jesus on Golgotha (Mark 15.29 par.Matt.27.40), worthy copies of biblical originals, the allusion simply takes up what we have read in the account of the session of the Sanhedrin, emphasizing the senseless presumption of such a suggestion.[42] The same dependence is suggested for Acts 6.14, an adaptation of what Luke has omitted in his own version of the trial.[43] There remains as a basic fact the report of the witnesses at the Jewish trial of Jesus: 'We heard him say, "I will destroy this temple that is made with hands, and in three days I will build another, not made with hands"' (Mark 14.58).[44]

Opinions vary over the origin of this saying. Several scholars think that it has been formed in stages. In addition to the two adjectives 'made with hands' (*chiropoiêtês*) and 'not made with hands' (*acheiropoiêtês*), the antiquity of which is suspect and to which we shall return, the rest can be split up. However, here differences of opinion arise as to which of the two parts is the earlier, not to mention whether either represents an authentic saying of Jesus: is it the positive part (Jesus will have announced the kingdom in the form of a metaphorical reconstruction of the temple) or the negative part, which stems from a saying about the destruction of the temple preserved in Mark 13.2, but which will have been modified?[45]

After what has been said earlier, we can exclude this latter proposition. It is in fact hard to see how the prophecy of the destruction of the temple could have been a threat in which Jesus gave himself the role of the destroyer; in other words, how an announcement of a classic, not to say conventional, kind could have been seen as a threat, apparently crazy and presumptuous, even if, when it was included in the account of the passion, it was defused by being placed on the lips of false witnesses.

So in our historical research, let us keep to the report of these witnesses. Without fear of being mistaken, we can extract from it the two adjectives 'made with hands' (*cheiropoiêtês*) and 'not made with hands' (*acheiropoiêtês*), which link up with other instances in the New Testament that resort to this same Greek vocabulary to denounce a form of worship which is henceforth obsolete.[46] The rest clearly proves not to have been retouched. A Christian creation *ex eventu* seems improbable. To suppose that this saying saw the light over the ruins of the temple, shortly after 70,[47] would ridicule Jesus, since the temple was not destroyed by him but by the Romans. We can add that in the account of the trial there was a concern to neutralize this very saying by the disagreement between the witnesses,[48] a sign that it was thought troublesome, though it nevertheless appeared in the tradition about the causes of the condemnation of Jesus.

What form did it take on his lips? It is very difficult to answer this question with any certainty. On the one hand, the version that we have has been formulated by accusers, which necessarily would lead them to emphasize its pretentiousness. On the other hand, we cannot believe that Jesus made such statements only once and in a single form: it is more than doubtful that a single saying pronounced before a few disciples would have been sufficient to spark off proceedings aimed at eliminating Jesus. At the least we must accept that Jesus announced the destruction and rebuilding of the temple, and that he gave himself a role in this double event. What role? It is impossible, in view of the state of our documentation, to give a certain answer to this question. At the most we can suggest that in the light of the mission that he attributed to himself in the face of the imminent kingdom of God, by his preaching he saw himself laying the foundations of a total renewal of the cult, which he could have expressed by several incisive formulae. The tenor of these would have been given by the 'false witnesses' at the trial.

Such statements can hardly have made him popular with the hierarchy in charge of the temple. Nor would they have made him popular with the general population, which was deeply attached to the temple and its rites, as is witnessed by the Jewish crowds who thronged to Jerusalem from Palestine and the Diaspora. Jesus gave the lie to this by expressing very different views of its future from that which delighted the pilgrim throng. No matter what his success may have been with the Galilean crowds, and accepting that he won the sympathy of the people of Jerusalem, these people as a whole could hardly have approved of any questioning of the sanctuary.[49] Such statements, particularly if made during the Passover, when the city was crammed with pilgrims,[50] would have exposed Jesus to opposition and denunciations, the latter in terms which we can easily imagine to have been exaggerated and therefore all the more dangerous. The result was the arrest of Jesus in Gethsemane by the priestly police.[51]

Was Jesus condemned for his criticism of the law?

Ferdinand Hahn[52] thinks that the members of the Sanhedrin, while fearing the political consequences of Jesus' attitude, based their proceedings principally on deliberate transgressions of the Law. Moreover, was not Jesus condemned as a blasphemer (Mark 14.64 par.)? Knowingly opposing the Law was blasphemy according to the Jewish legal system.

Several objections can be made to this interpretation of the facts. The first is that in the Gospel account of the session of the Sanhedrin at which Jesus was judged, the accusation of blasphemy does not relate to any kind of opposition to the Torah but to pretensions of quite another character. Another difficulty is that even accepting that this account has kept blasphemy as the main accusation while applying it to another charge than that to which it originally related, it does not seem that the position of Jesus on certain points of the Law could have merited such an accusation.

Among the definitions of blasphemy which can be found among the rabbis, the only one which could have applied here is the one which talks of 'speaking disrespectfully of the Law'.[53] Now of the statements of Jesus reported in the Gospels, very few could be criticized for this. That could not be the case in the declaration that 'the sabbath is made for man, not man for the sabbath' (Mark 2.27), a maxim which has parallels in the rabbis. The position taken by Jesus over ritual purity is bolder, if it is true that Jesus 'declared all foods pure' (Mark 7.19b) and uttered the magisterial statement that 'there is nothing outside a man which by going into him can defile him; but the things which come out of a man are what defile him' (Mark 7.15). But these words appear only in the Gospel of Mark and in part in Matthew, who depends on Mark. Nothing similar appears in the so-called 'second Synoptic source' (Q)[54] on which Matthew and Luke draw and which includes above all sayings of Jesus. This conclusion about the statements quoted probably puts us in a non-Palestinian Christian milieu, Gentile–Christian or mixed. At all events questions about food and the sabbath were more likely to arise in such a situation than in churches in which these things still remained a matter of routine, even if there was negligence in the practice of them.[55]

It is true that in announcing the end of temple worship Jesus was making obsolete legislation which to a considerable degree consisted in regulations for such worship. But Jesus never contrasted two 'norms', one related to sacrificial worship as practised in the Jerusalem temple and the other to establishing a relationship with God without this worship,[56] as if one were bad and the other good. What he will have indicated, in words and actions, is that the present form of the cult was transitory and had to come to an end because of the advent of a new and definitive order. Similarly, Jesus could have been condemned for his views on the temple without being accused of challenging the Torah. The latter could still have been valid in his eyes while the present order lasted.

Whatever we make of these relationships and inferences, there is nothing in the accounts of the trial of Jesus which leads us to suspect that these standpoints on the Law and its precepts played the slightest role in his arrest and death.[57] But there is an additional reason for excluding a motif of this kind from Jesus' 'file', and beyond doubt this is the most important. It is that neither the hierarchy nor the Sanhedrin over which it presided had were concerned with such questions. An adventurous exegesis of the Torah, reforming views about its application, too personal a *halakhah* were all reasons for Jesus to have been investigated, if that was his position, but not by the priestly authorities in Jerusalem. These controlled the strictly political order and touched on religious subjects only where they had a political relevance. Had Jesus been suspected or accused of matters relating to the Law and its interpretation, he would have appeared before a rabbinic tribunal, a *bêt dîn* presided over by legal experts. Had he been condemned, these would have inflicted the thirty-nine blows of the whip which the 'heretic' Paul boasts that he had received five times (II Cor.11.24). Perhaps they might have excommunicated him, but Jesus would not have died the death of crucifixion under the Romans after being denounced by the hierocrats. For that, he would have had to have been a threat to public order. Now that was the case if Jesus, with his criticisms of the temple and its worship, and surrounded by disciples in whom he inculcated his views of the future, had begun to cause trouble among the population, at the height of the Passover pilgrimage.

An action by the Pharisees?

As I have remarked, Jesus' views on the temple could not have pleased the people, far less its leaders or its religious guides.

However, among the latter, members of the Pharisaic movement are absent from the account of the passion according to Mark. They appear in the accounts by the other Gospels[58] only by way of exception and as indubitable witnesses to the anti-Jewish polemic after 70, when the Pharisees occupied the highest circles of Judaism. As for the scribes or doctors of the law, for the most part Pharisees, we find them in these same accounts only in session in the Sanhedrin,[59] where no specific role is attributed to them.

This state of affairs matches what we can know of Jesus' earlier relationships with these groups. Apart from the mysterious sentence about the 'leaven of the Pharisees',[60] the Gospel texts, despite appearances, hardly favour an opposition between the historical Jesus and the movement.

One curious thing is that the Gospels which dissociate the Pharisees furthest from the account of the Passion are those in which their role as types of adversaries of Jesus is stated most clearly in his public ministry, namely the Gospels of Mark and John. In the other Gospels, the attacks made by the scribes and/or Pharisees, and in which they take the initiative, are a legacy of Mark, the exceptions simply coming from the pen of the evangelists.[61] Now these attacks generally give us the impression of being a literary creation, the aim of which is to give Jesus the opportunity to make pronouncements or issue polemic on various positions (thus in Mark 11.27–12.37). These facts are completed by what we know of Jewish persecution in the first days of the church: none of the murders of which Christians were victims before 70 presupposes the responsibility of the Pharisees as such. Neither the stoning of Stephen (Acts 6.8–15; 7.59–60) nor the execution of James the son of Zebedee (Acts 12.2) nor that of James the 'brother of the Lord'[62] is blamed on them, and the last example involves the priestly aristocracy as in the case of Jesus.

Certainly to the degree that the Sanhedrin was involved, the Pharisees cannot be eliminated: but all the facts in our possession indicate beyond any possible doubt where in the last resort those responsible are to be found.

4

Jesus before the Jewish Authorities

The facts in the Gospels

Mark (14.53) and Luke (22.54) report that Jesus, after being captured by the troop, was taken to the high priest's house. So does Matthew (26.57), who adds the detail that this high priest was called Caiaphas. John (18.13,24) goes his own way: according to him the guards first bring Jesus to the house of Annas, father-in-law of Caiaphas, before taking him to the latter.

The events which follow are identical in the first two Gospels (Mark 14.53b–72; Matt.26.57b–75). Hardly has Jesus arrived in the high priest's palace than the Sanhedrin gathers and there is a session of the tribunal at which Jesus is judged and condemned to death: it is followed by a scene in which Jesus is insulted, followed by Peter's denials. Everything takes place by night. In the morning there is a meeting of the Sanhedrin at the end of which Jesus is sent to Pilate (Mark 15.1; Matt.27.1–2). According to Luke (22.63–23.1) Jesus is guarded throughout the night in the house of the high priest by minions who maltreat him. During this period, Peter denies his master. It is only at daybreak that the Sanhedrin gathers and there is the session which Mark and Matthew put during the night. After this Jesus is led before Pilate. Finally John (18.19–24, 28) knows of no intervention on the part of the Sanhedrin: according to him, Jesus undergoes an interrogation by Annas and is then taken to Caiaphas. We do not know what happens during this second stage, but from there he is brought before Pilate. Here Peter's denials are arranged in such a way that the first precedes the interrogation and the two other follow the transfer to Caiaphas, thus providing the framework for Jesus' appearance before the Jewish authorities.

The session of the Sanhedrin according to the Synoptic Gospels

Before we weigh up the external arguments for or against the historicity of the session of the Sanhedrin at which Jesus was judged, we must look at the texts which describe it and, behind their final redaction, investigate the traditions that they bring together so that we can evaluate their historical value.[1]

Mark's version (14.53–64)[2] is a composite whole. We can see this from the beginning, since the scene only begins after the following scene has been intimated: by introducing Peter into the palace of the high priest (14.54), Mark prepares for his denials (14.66–72). We know that he likes to slip a story into a sequence:[3] moreover, the two episodes form a kind of diptych which makes the reader ask: 'Jesus has already made his confession – will the disciple, like Peter, be a renegade, or imitate his master and confess his faith?'[4]

But the text also shows other signs of retouching. The main one is to be found in v.59: the witnesses who have just reported the words of Jesus about the temple could hardly have been clearer and there is not the slightest trace of disagreement. However, the text goes on to tell us that 'on this their testimony did not agree'. After that comes a question from the high priest: 'Have you no answer to make? What is it that these men testify against you?' (v.60), a question which is almost inexplicable, since because their evidence is contradictory, it is of no value. Things become different if we detach v.59: after the discordant depositions of the first witnesses (v.56), the accusation is more precise and becomes overwhelming: it is Jesus' saying about the temple. But Jesus does not offer any reply to this accusation, here conforming to the model presented by Holy Scripture.[5] At the same time he is saving himself for another type of acknowledgment, which the high priest is going to require of him in person and which alone will decide his fate.

That must have been the original narrative,[6] before some well-intentioned but clumsy retouching damaged it: by adding v.59 on the disagreement of the witnesses, the last redactor wanted to neutralize the saying about the temple. It is also at this level that we should put the alignment of the second deposition upon the first, so that everything becomes false witness, here again along the lines of the prophecies in the Old Testament.[7]

The second question of the high priest changes key, with, 'Are you the Christ, the Son of the Blessed?' (v.61). In his reply, Jesus uses a synonym of this latter title, which is a metonym translated from the Hebrew, namely 'Power': an equivalent to the sacred tetragrammaton and a further indication of a Semitic original. The messianic question is answered in the same terms. The reply is complete affirmative and is developed[8] in an eschatological and apocalyptic perspective in which we glimpse the hope of the final return of Christ the Son of Man. Here is a combination of two scriptural passages[9] which lie at the heart of the most traditional testimonies applied to Jesus by the apostolic church.

The high priest cries 'Blasphemy!', and we can understand this when we realize that Jesus' reply is none other than the confession of faith of the first Christians. For a Jew, to declare oneself Messiah is not a blasphemy. But things are different if a man claims to be Son of God in the Christian sense of the title and his followers acknowledge him as such.[10] We can see the consequences: this dialogue is Christian; it is an *ad hoc* composition aimed at bringing out the mystery of Christ the Son of God, uniting in his person the glory of the divinity and a destiny which consigns him to suffering and death.

But the whole scene derives from a Christian hand.[11] For in reality this 'trial' is in fact a kind of christological compendium provided for the believing reader to reflect on: Jesus, whose divine glory is now disguised under the ignominious veil of the passion, will make it shine forth at the time of his imminent triumph for the well-being of his followers and the shame of his enemies.

In fact, there is little in this narrative which can be said to have a historical origin. Only the threat to destroy the temple has its roots in the sayings of Jesus, as I demonstrated in the previous chapter. That is the case in Mark, and neither Matthew nor Luke offer any additional support at the historical level. The former (26.59–66) recasts the Markan narrative. As for Luke

(22.66–71), whether or not he depends only on Mark,[12] his account has no historical verisimilitude, for what he describes is in no way a session of the tribunal, and everything combines here to instruct the reader, through the very 'mouth' of Jesus, in the titles and qualities of the one who is undergoing the passion.

The Johannine version

If we cannot count on Matthew and Luke to make up for the defects in Mark relating to the Jewish proceedings against Jesus, the Gospel of John would appear at first sight to come to the aid of the historian with a very different version of events from what one reads in the three others. Here there is no session of the Sanhedrin, but on the very night of the arrest there is an interrogation of Jesus at the house of Annas, the father-in-law of Caiaphas, followed by an appearance before the latter. However, this version should not arouse false hopes, since it is less original than one might think.

Certainly, we can grant that the evangelist drew from traditional recollections that Jesus was taken to Annas. There is a connection between Annas and Caiaphas in the Gospel of Luke (3.2) and in the Acts of the Apostles (4.6), as C.H.Dodd aptly remarks: 'It seems highly improbable that John should have dug out the names from remote passages of the Lukan writings to adorn his narrative.'[13] Dodd goes on to note the clumsiness in this note in the Fourth Gospel[14] and draws the following conclusion from it, which one can only endorse: 'An author composing freely would not be so likely to allow himself to fall into this kind of confusion as one who was incorporating material which, at a distance in space and time, he did not fully understand.'

That having been said, the course of the interrogation reported in John 18.19–23 can no more be derived from historical information than the Synoptic account of the session of the Sanhedrin. We can recognize that an enquiry about 'the disciples of Jesus and his teaching' is not inconceivable on the part of a hierarch.[15] However, the enquiry is there only to introduce a reply from Jesus (18.21), from which it is inseparable. Now this reply and what follows bear all the traces of a composition by the evangelist, in which probable recollections of the Synoptics are swallowed up in a passage which essentially presents Johannine themes and expressions.

The reminder that Jesus taught in 'the synagogue and the temple' without being apprehended (18.20) evokes the almost identical declaration of Jesus in Gethsemane in Mark 14.49.[16] 'One of the guards' (*hypêretôn*) gives Jesus a blow (*rhapisma*) as in Mark 14.65; the 'guards' or the 'servants' (*hyperetai*) likewise rain 'blows' (*rhapismasin*) on him. The whole passage is full of recollections of the public activity of Jesus as this is described in John, and once more we have John's theological and polemical themes.[17] A series of expressions bears his signature: 'speak openly' (*parrhesia lalein*) and the noun *parrhesia* itself; 'in the world', 'in synagogue' (without the article) and 'in secret' (*en kryptoi*, without the article), 'the Jews', 'bear witness' (*martyrein*), a typically Johannine verb, above all when followed by the preposition *peri* (never in the New Testament outside John and I John).

Some scholars have seen the transfer to Caiaphas as a vestige of the Sanhedrin session. Although John shows that he knew this last,[18] the explanation is doubtful, since Caiaphas appears only in the Matthaean version and it is hard to understand why John should have taken it from there to produce this appendix in which nothing happens.[19] Rather, John depends on a tradition which has added a second session, with Caiaphas, to the appearance of Jesus before Annas in order to make the affair official, since it was known that Caiaphas was the high priest in office at that time. Aware of the traditional nature of this note, John thought it good to preserve it, though it did not add much to his narrative.

Two facts emerge from the previous examination which merit further study. These are, independently of the statements made in each case, the appearance of Jesus before Annas and his judgment by the Sanhedrin.

Jesus before Annas

Ḥanan, Graecized into Annas in the New Testament and Ananos in Josephus, was the only high priest nominated by Quirinius, legate of Syria, after the deposition of Archelaus in 6 CE. His high priesthood lasted until 15, but was then so to speak extended, since five of his sons and one of his grandsons were high priests.[20] However, the most famous of the members of Annas's family to accede to this position was his son-in-law, Joseph Qayyafa,[21] our Caiaphas. Such permanence says a lot about the power and influence of his figure. If the reputation of his line is clearly a bad one in Jewish tradition, which criticizes him for his nepotism, his exactions and his brutality, we have to acknowledge that the family and its head had a proven eye for the main chance, since we know that at this time the high priest held his post at the discretion of the Roman governor, who nominated him and deposed him at well.[22] That was particularly true of Caiaphas, who remained in office for nineteen years, from 18 to 37, whereas the average length of the twenty-eight last high priests was only four years. On being nominated in 26, Pilate hastened to confirm Caiaphas in his office, an office which he held until the end of Pilate's time as prefect in 36 – proof that the two men were cronies. The object of the hostility of the one, Jesus could hardly escape that of the other.

Since Caiaphas was high priest in office when Jesus was seized, he bears the ultimate official responsibility for the action. However, it is not surprising that Jesus was taken before Annas, since at that time the latter continued to exert some moral power over the whole hierarchy. Might he not have taken the initiative in launching the operation with the agreement of his son-in-law? At least that is a possibility.

However, there was no legal necessity for Jesus to be taken to him, and to talk in this connection of a 'preliminary interrogation' does not accord with any form of Jewish procedure.[23] Was this move something that the police thought convenient, or a request from Annas, who was curious to see the dangerous prophet in person? We can only guess.

The meeting took place 'with Annas', in other words at his home, if this is how we are to understand the expression *pros Hannan* in John 18.13, which is perfectly correct. Despite pious localizations,[24] it is impossible to discover where Annas lived. At all events, it has not been established that, as has sometimes been claimed, he lived in a wing of the high priest's palace, and in any case this latter building has not been located.[25]

Was Jesus judged by the Sanhedrin?

What corresponds in John to the nocturnal session of the Sanhedrin in the Gospels of Mark and Matthew is the presentation of Jesus to Annas (not his transfer to the house of Caiaphas). However, John knew this episode, since he recalls it at other points in his Gospel.[26] If he omits it in the account of the passion, it is because for him the public debates with the Jews are in practice over by the end of chapter 12, where Jesus pronounces his definitive sayings about the Jews.

Here we must first look at the evidence in the Synoptic Gospels about the judgment of Jesus by the supreme council of the nation. This fact, which appears for the first time in Mark, is not an invention of the author. While it is not necessary to confirm it by citing Luke 22.66–71 and envisaging the use in this passage of a source different for Mark – a recourse which is very doubtful[27] – it is clear that the Markan account is taking up and retouching an earlier composition, the origin of which is to be put at the Semitic stage of the Gospel traditions. Although Christian in origin and content, as has been demonstrated above, this narrative touches on basic facts the historicity of which cannot be challenged *a priori*.

However, in Mark (followed by Matthew), this factual basis is broken up, indeed split. The nocturnal session is followed in the morning by an action on the part of the Sanhedrin which results in Jesus being sent to Pilate (Mark 15.1). But to whom are we to attribute this note? And first of all, what does it mean?

The reply to the second question depends on the meaning to be given to the expressions *symboulion poiêsantes* (variant *etoimasantes*) in Mark 15.1 and *symboulion elabon* in Matt.27.1. Making up for rapid and superficial pieces of lexicography, Pierre Benoit[28] has made an in-depth study of these phrases in Greek literature and in the New Testament. He concludes that *symboulion* never means 'decision', 'resolution'. In all the documents in which it is to be found this word, 'formed at a late stage to correspond to the Latin *consilium* . . . denotes a "council", that is to say a deliberative assembly, whether as the body that has been constituted or in the very act of deliberation'.[29] We can see the consequences: whatever the verb used in Mark 15.1 and Matt.27.1, we have a new session, different from the one held at night, and not just the conclusion, in the early morning, of the nocturnal audience.

But what is the value of the note for the tradition, not to mention its historical value? There are some traces of Markan redaction.[30] However, the term 'redaction' does not imply *a priori* creation pure and simple. Why should have Mark split the session? There is nothing to suggest that he saw some irregularity in the nocturnal judgment. Nor is there in Mark 15.1, which indicates a second session intended to endorse the first: if only Mark had written that the members of the Sanhedrin sat 'again' (*palin*), resorting to his favourite adverb! But no, everything happens as though the first session had never taken place. Certainly Mark could have wanted to mark a climax (the end of the Jewish trial), hence the emphasis on the presentation, which introduces 'the high priests with the elders and the scribes and all the Sanhedrin'. But this is only to formalize a fact which we have every reason to believe to be part of the tradition. Mark utilized it to the utmost, although it was not necessary for his composition. Luke (22.66) equally exploits it by fixing his one session of the Sanhedrin in the morning.[31]

Unlike the nocturnal session, which makes double use of the tradition about the audience with Annas, in the morning session we have a pocket of resistance which is very difficult to reduce. Bultmann[32] saw it as the traditional nucleus of the account in Mark 14.55–64 and there is no difficulty in adopting this point of view. The memory of a nocturnal appearance of Jesus before and 'at the house of *a* high priest' (Annas bore this title) gave rise to an audience before the supreme council 'at the house of *the* high priest' (Mark 14.53).

These conclusions have been formulated solely on the basis of the Gospel texts, which I have taken care to compare and subject to a critical examination. They have the advantage of resolving problems and providing an answer to certain classical objections, for example the place where the trial is thought to have taken place. No document indicates the dwelling of the high priest as the place where the Sanhedrin met.[33] However, that is what is implied by Mark 14.53, where the expression *pros ton archierea* is normally understood in this sense according to the context; in the following verse Peter is said to go 'inside the palace' of the high priest (14.54).[34] Now the laborious efforts of scholars to resolve the incompatibility between the archaeological facts and those in the Gospels no longer have any *raison d'être* as soon as we dismiss the nocturnal session of the Sanhedrin as unhistorical and accept that in reality Jesus was simply presented to Annas, in his own home. The same reply can be given to those who recall that according to the Mishnah, criminal trials could only be held in the daytime, or when it is claimed that there were no witnesses capable of reporting the statements made during the audience.[35]

Waiting for morning: Jesus in the hands of the servants

The Gospel narratives of the passion contain two scenes involving insults of which Jesus is the victim. One comes within the framework of the Jewish procedure, the other in its Roman counterpart. This latter episode can be found in Mark (15.16–20), Matthew (27.27–31) and John (19.2–3). Luke omits it, but has kept traces of it in the interlude with Herod (22.11). The first scene is reported by Mark (14.65), Matthew (16.67–68) and Luke (22.63–65). As we have seen,[36] John probably echoes it in 18.22. Although these two episodes are very similar and lend themselves to some contamination, there is no need to derive them for a single original event. On the one hand, there are more

differences than similarities, and on the other the respective
details correspond to different types of situation.

For the moment, let us consider the first scene. The account
that Mark gives us (14.65) is in fact disordered: Jesus is spat
upon, his face is veiled, he is struck, he is asked to prophesy – all
this by 'certain' members of the Sanhedrin; by way of an
appendix we are told that the 'servants' intervene in turn.
Matthew (26.67–68) brings some order to his source: Jesus no
longer seems to be struck on a veiled face (this feature is
suppressed) and the blows are only mentioned once. Luke
(22.64–65) particularly stands out in offering an attenuated
version along the line which he follows elsewhere in describing
the passion: relieving Jesus of as much humiliation and scorn as
possible. Here there is no spitting, and if Jesus receives blows,
Luke leaves them rather vague. On the other hand, Jesus is put in
the forefront by a connection between this scene and the
prophecies of the passion (Luke 18.32 with the word *empaizein*,
as in 22.63) and the description 'blasphemy' for the insults.

Despite its defects, the Markan version is freest from retouching, and we must begin from it in evaluating the historicity of the
scene. The contribution of the Old Testament (Isa.50.6)[37] is
indisputable here, but that does not exclude the possibility that
the facts are real. We must remember that the evangelists are not
accustomed to dwell on the details of the passion which infringe
the infinite dignity of the one who is undergoing it. If they do so
here, it is because they had an opportunity to illustrate a parallel
with the prophecies, for the instruction of their readers.

On the other hand, we must dismiss the idea that members of
the Sanhedrin took part in this vulgar scene. Yet that is what we
read in Mark, and Matthew reinforces him, implying that all the
supreme council are involved without distinction, and not
mentioning the servants. Luke attributes everything solely to the
latter and there is no problem in following him if we accept, as we
have just done, that the nocturnal session of the Sanhedrin is
totally unhistorical. The situation is completely fictitious: it was
in some outbuilding or, doubtless better, in the court of Annas's
house, that Jesus, under guard until daybreak, was handed over

to the brutality of the servants.[38] The objection that there would have been no witnesses to such a scene bears no weight: at that time eastern customs allowed more freedom of access to the great than our police rules do today.

One could also think either of a report by the anonymous disciple mentioned in John 18.15–16, to the degree that he is to be seen as a real figure,[39] or by Peter. At all events, the presence of the chief of the apostles here and his denials, leaving aside the artifice with which they are arranged in the Gospel accounts, are quite probable. It is by no means impossible that Peter, in the course of this dark affair, should have been driven by curiosity[40] (and perhaps by some remorse) to go near to Annas's house, where, after being identified, he became afraid and denied all contact with Jesus. It would in fact be astonishing if a Christian had made up, as a deterrent to potential apostates, a story which imputed such behaviour to the eminent figure of Peter, the first witness to the resurrection and who was venerated as a martyr at the time of the Gospels, if it did not have a basis in reality.[41] But the substance of the note is valuable and, once we accept that its location in this text conforms with history – and there is nothing against this – it allows us to see how the Christian communities got wind of one of the most repugnant aspects of the passion, when Jesus was delivered over the whim and sadism of un-scrupulous servants.

The morning meeting of the Sanhedrin

A session of the Sanhedrin took place on the morning following Jesus' arrest: at least that is what a study of the texts and the underlying traditions has allowed us to accept.

Although this assembly was convened by the high priest, it did not take place in the latter's palace, as the Gospels of Mark and Matthew suggest[42] (Mark 14.53; Matt.26.57, for the nocturnal session that they relate), but in an appropriate locality. Unfortunately the documents do not help us to be as precise as we would like, and opinions on this subject vary considerably. When he is describing the ancient rampart of Jerusalem to the north,

Josephus puts the council chamber (*boulê,* elsewhere also *bouleutêrion*) to the east of the Xystos, the great market place linked by a bridge to the Temple Mount, and west of it. It can be taken as certain that this council chamber was outside the upper city (on the western hill, west of the Tyropoeon), since Josephus notes that at the capture of Jerusalem the building was burned before the Romans had reached this part of the city.[43] One would like to know whether it was inside or outside the temple precinct. The Mishnah[44] indicates a place called *lishkat ha-gazît* as the place where the Sanhedrin sat, south of the Court of the Priests. This term, which is usually translated 'room of cut stones' and sometimes 'room of the paving stones', can also be understood in the sense of 'room of [near to] the Xystos'.[45] The location given by the Mishnah leaves much to be desired, for it is hard to see how a room in the Court of the Priests could have had any other than a liturgical use. On the other hand, according to the last translation mentioned, the nomenclature, which certainly applies for the time of Josephus, can reinforce the view that the council chamber was on the temple forecourt, i.e. bordering it to the south-west.[46]

What took place at the morning meeting? No document recalls this, and there were no witnesses to leak the discussions. We only know the result: Jesus was led before Pilate. We need not imagine the formal session of a tribunal. On the other hand, we can conceive that the high priests thought it advisable to involve their partners in the Sanhedrin, or at least some of them, in on the enterprise, and that together they examined the case of Jesus (perhaps with others),[47] at least to frame the charges to be presented to Pilate. If that is the case, we have met the objection that recalls the prohibition, formulated in the Mishnah, against proceeding to judicial debates on the eve of the sabbath or a feast day, which would apply both to the Synoptic chronology (Jesus crucified on a Friday, the day of the Passover) and that of the Fourth Gospel (Jesus crucified on a Friday, the eve of the Passover).[48] For there is nothing in the text which obliges us to suppose any exception to a rule thought already to be in force at the time of Jesus. In my view, the most certain conclusion is that Jesus only had to face a Roman trial.

5

The Roman Trial

If the Jewish authorities made arrangements to transfer Jesus to the Roman tribunal, it was because they either did not want to or could not settle the final fate of the accused themselves. It is not even certain that they passed sentence on him, since, as we have seen, the account which mentions this (Mark 14.64. par Matt.26.66)[1] is a development by Christians of the report of an informal audience in the house of Annas, who himself had no judicial power as an individual. Whatever form the morning meeting may have taken, it is beyond question that Jesus was condemned to death by Pontius Pilate. On this point the evidence of the New Testament is confirmed by that of Tacitus, who, reporting the execution of the Christians of Rome on the order of Nero, explains that their name comes from 'Christus' who suffered the extreme penalty during the reign of 'Tiberius at the hand of one of our procurators, Pontius Pilate'.[2] We may add an equally undisputed fact: Jesus was crucified. Now this form of execution was Roman, not Jewish, at least in the period with which we are concerned,[3] and that presupposes that it was carried out on the orders of the Roman authorities. Had Jesus been put to death by Jewish executioners on the orders of a Jewish tribunal, he would have been stoned.

The rights of the Sanhedrin

But why Pontius Pilate? In other words, why didn't the Jewish authorities themselves proceed to execute Jesus? The Gospel of John gives an answer through the mouth of the very people who

wanted to do away with him: 'We have no right to put anyone to
death' (18.31). This reply is accepted for various reasons by a
large number of scholars whom we need not note by name.[4] Here
are some conclusions which summarize the results of the most
recent work.

First of all some general remarks[5] about the political situation
in Judaea at that time. On the accession of Herod the Great to the
throne in 40 BCE the Sanhedrin, the supreme council of the
Jewish nation, had lost the authority which it had enjoyed in the
time of the Hasmoneans. From now on the ancestral laws had
given place to a new regime, that of the *rex socius* of the Roman
empire.[6] The Jewish authorities exercised what remained of local
law only as a concession. The situation was the same under direct
Roman administration, when Judaea became a Roman province
of the third class, ruled by a governor[7] of equestrian rank. Local
law, and especially penal law, existed only in the form of
privileges graciously granted by the Roman authorities. Can we
include the right to carry out death sentences among these
privileges?

On this basis, some scholars have claimed that the Jewish trial
of Jesus can be said to be totally unhistorical. Supposing that the
Sanhedrin had had the freedom to put Jesus to death, it would
have had to do so by stoning. Now Jesus was crucified, a Roman
punishment. So it is concluded that there was no Jewish trial, and
that the account of it in the Gospels is a fiction.[8] However, no
matter what reasons there may be for coming to this conclusion
(see the preceding chapter), the basic question just mentioned,
namely whether the Sanhedrin had the right to execute capital
sentences, needs to be examined.

Some evidence in rabbinic literature suggests that jurisdiction
in matters involving death sentences was exercised by the
Sanhedrin down to the destruction of the temple.[9] It is most
probable here that the senior Jewish clergy of the time had been
convinced that they had this power. But to what degree was this
certainty translated into real practice? To answer that question
we need to recall a series of facts some years nearer to those which
concern us.[10]

The first is the stoning of James, 'brother of the Lord', and some other Christians on the authority of the high priest Ananus (Ḥanan) II. As Josephus writes:

> He thought he had now a proper opportunity. Festus was now dead, and Albinus was but upon the road. So he assembled the Sanhedrin of judges, and brought before them the brother of Jesus who was called Christ, whose name was James, and some others. And when he had formed an accusation against them as breakers of the law, he delivered them to be stoned. But those who seemed the most equitable of the citizens, and accurate in legal matters, disliked what was done. They also sent to King Agrippa, desiring him to send to Ananus that he should act so no more; for that what he had already done was not to be justified. Indeed, some of them went also to meet Albinus, as he was upon his journey from Alexandria, and informed him that it was not lawful for Ananus to assemble a Sanhedrin without his consent. Albinus was persuaded by what they said, and wrote in anger to Ananus, and threatened that he would bring him to punishment for what he had done. On which account King Agrippa took the high priesthood from him when he had ruled only three months, and made Jesus the son of Damneus high priest. [11]

This text is not very clear, and without doubt contains some inaccuracies. It reports two interventions with different motives. The first intervention is with Agrippa and points out the illegality of what he had already done (*to prôton*). Josephus does not say what this is, but we may follow David Catchpole, [12] who proceeds by a process of elimination, excluding both the convening of the Sanhedrin – which these pious Jews could not regard as an illegality – and the execution of James and his companions, the last act and not the 'first' in the affair. There remains the illegality of the judgment itself, and this fits the previous context, in which Josephus is emphasizing the harshness of the Sadducees in exercising justice. Thus the first intervention. The second, that with Albinus, is motivated according to Josephus by the fact that the high priest could not convene the Sanhedrin without the authority of the procurator. This notice is curious for two reasons: first, that the Jews seem to be instructing Albinus on his own prerogatives, and secondly that only the *convening* of the Sanhedrin is said to be a matter for the local Roman authorities. It is quite plausible that Josephus is wrong in both matters, and in the case of the second it would be wrong to deduce from his text, as some scholars have done, that the Sanhedrin, having met with the permission of the procurator, was then free to act at will, including decreeing and executing death sentences. As Jean-Pierre Lémonon notes,[13] 'in fact the whole of the text emphasizes that Ananus profited from the vacancy in the office of procurator to hand James and some others over to the Sanhedrin and have them stoned. It is clear that if the Sanhedrin had full powers in matters relating to capital punishment, Josephus would not have emphasized so strongly that Ananus thought that this vacancy gave him a favourable opportunity.'

Another example[14] comes a little later, under the procuratorship of the same Albinus (62–64), when a poor peasant, Jesus son of Ananias, begins to run round Jerusalem crying: 'A voice from the east, a voice from the west, a voice from the four winds, a voice against Jerusalem and the temple, a voice against husband and wife (Jer.7.34), a voice against all the people!' The man was arrested on the orders of 'citizens of note', who made him run the gauntlet; then these same 'magistrates' took him before Albinus. The latter had him flogged 'to the bone' as a means of torture, but at every blow the man received he only repeated his oracle of misfortune. Judging him mad, Albinus had him released.[15] The 'citizens of note' or 'the magistrates' are none other than the members of the Sanhedrin, who in the event could only have planned to execute this figure. His case also evokes that of another Jesus since, in addition to the homonymy, the affair was sparked off by a religious crime, in this case an oracle against the temple. Above all, in both cases the pronouncement of the death sentence fell to the procurator, following the wishes of the Jewish authorities, who had lost their power.

This restriction of the power of the Sanhedrin is confirmed by a series of rabbinic passages.[16] What arises from them in connection with our concern can be summed up in a few words: forty years before the destruction of the temple, the Sanhedrin lost its powers in capital matters. That brings us to the time of Pilate (26–36). No fact of this nature is indicated for this period in the sources, especially in Josephus, and we may see the forty years as a round figure indicating a period of more than a generation, which goes back to 6 CE, when direct Roman administration was inaugurated in Judaea.

A number of other facts seem to run contrary to these indications, but do not in fact do them great damage.

First of all there is the martyrdom of Stephen according to the Acts of the Apostles (7.55–8.3), an improbable scene in which we see the members of the Sanhedrin pouncing on Stephen and leading him off to punishment. There is no sentence, but without any doubt the echo of a lynching on which the author of Acts wants to confer a juridical veneer in the form of an execution by the supreme council of the Jews.[17]

Another case mentioned in the same book of the New Testament (Acts 12.2) is that of James, son of Zebedee, who was put to death on the orders of Herod Agrippa I in a period (31–44) when procuratorial rule in Judaea was interrupted. It was also in the reign of this Agrippa that a priest's daughter was executed for prostitution: she had bundles of wood piled up round her and was burned.[18]

Then comes the threat against the Gentiles who dared to enter the temple precinct. This prohibition is indicated by Philo and, twice, by Josephus.[19] In the *Jewish War*, the speech which he attributes to Titus contains criticisms which allude to the barrier separating the Court of the Gentiles from the rest of the temple which bore an inscription in Greek and Latin threatening death to non-Jews who crossed it, a threat formulated with the agreement of the Romans. Titus refers to it like this: 'Have not we ourselves given you every freedom to do away with those who cross [this barrier], even if [the delinquent] were a Roman?' Moreover Josephus also mentions this 'stone barrier' on which 'an inscription prohibited entry to strangers on pain of death'.[20] This inscription has been confirmed by archaeology thanks to its discovery by C.Clermont-Ganneau in 1871. A second similar inscription was published by J.H.Iliffe in 1938.[21] According to the translation proposed by the archaeologist, the first inscription with the prohibition reads as follows: 'No foreigner is to enter within the forecourt and the balustrade around the sanctuary. Whoever is caught will have himself to blame for his subsequent death.'[22] Karlheinz Müller has questioned how free the Jews will have been to put the transgressor to death without going through Roman justice. This is, first, because Josephus includes even Roman citizens in the threat and they enjoyed certain legal privileges, and secondly, because no text suggests that this was lynch law. That suggests a regular trial, which in the case of Gentiles could only have been ordered by the Roman authorities. However, Josephus' terms are in fact clear: this is a privilege granted to the *Jews*, who have received the right to put to death Gentiles guilty of violating the sanctuary. Since in such a case there was no question of a Jewish trial, the only alternative is lynch law. In other words, 'if the guilty party is lynched, the Romans will not intervene'.[23] So the example that we have just examined provides no evidence of any right that the Sanhedrin may have had to proceed to executions on capital charges.

We can therefore dismiss the thesis that 'before 70 CE the Sanhedrin had full jurisdiction over Jews accused of transgressions against the Jewish religious law and had the authority to pronounce death sentences and implement them freely in conformity with the dispositions of Jewish legislation'.[24] In reality, not only did the Sanhedrin have no authority to implement a death sentence, but any death sentence that it could have passed was invalid in the eyes of the Roman authorities. It is politically inconceivable that the Romans would have been content merely to implement the decisions of a Jewish tribunal. If the Jews, unwilling to assassinate an undesirable character, resorted to the Romans to get rid of him, the Romans could only act on their own responsibility and institute a Roman trial.

The Gospel accounts

The appearance of Jesus before Pilate's tribunal is related in the four Gospels.[25] None of the four versions can be regarded as an exact account of the facts.

Leaving aside the Barabbas episode, to which we shall return, Mark's account (15.2–15) has many historical improbabilities. It begins abruptly, without an accusation or any indication of why Pilate should have asked Jesus whether he was 'king of the Jews'. We are surprised not to note any reaction from Pilate after Jesus has acknowledged[26] his claim to this title, which would normally be tantamount to high treason, and to see Pilate continuing the session as though nothing important had happened. In the end there is no sentence, but a capitulation on the part of the governor, who abandons Jesus 'to please the crowd'. This account, the character of which resembles that of the Sanhedrin session,[27] is full of christological, apologetic and indeed polemical themes, which go far beyond an objective account of the course of a trial.

Luke's version (Luke 23.2–5) has one special feature which will strike any reader: the session is interrupted by an interlude in which Jesus is presented to Herod Antipas (Luke 23.7–12). This is quite a significant feature which we shall have to examine carefully later. The rest of the narrative offers no more opportunities to the historian than the parallel account in Mark, for which Luke is either dependent on Mark or which he derives from another source.[28] The explicit accusation of subversion is a way in which this author, concerned to provided a logical narrative, fills the gap which we note in all the other versions.[29] The charges laid out in Luke 23.2 and summarized in other terms in v.6 are deliberately explicit and unadorned in order to bring out all the more clearly what a slender case is made by Pilate, since three times he emphasizes Jesus' innocence and hence the emptiness of similar accusations.[30]

Matthew, whose account (27.11–26) is dependent on Mark, adds two episodes to Mark: one is the intervention of Pilate's wife in favour of the accused (27.19); the other is the scene in which

Pilate declines all responsibility by washing his hands in front of the crowd, which responds by taking responsibility for the death of Jesus (27.24–25). Neither of these two additions has any historical value: Pilate's wife talks as if she were a Jew, and Pilate is following scripture: the whole passages is steeped in biblical and Matthaean themes.[31]

In its account of the Roman trial the Fourth Gospel (18.28–19.16a) offers us a beautifully constructed composition of deep theological significance. It has several points in common with Mark, which seriously raises the question of dependence. Moreover the anti-Jewish and no less anti-Roman focus (Pilate is rejected, as belonging to the category of 'world') suggests the experience of a church which has already suffered a twofold rejection and a twofold persecution.[32] However, the account offers the historian some unique facts: not only the echo, already indicated, of the limits imposed on the power of the Sanhedrin (18.31), but also two details, one chronological (18.28; 19.14) and the other topographical (19.13), which we shall be utilizing in due course.

Historical conclusions

High priests and crowd

The role of the high priests in presenting Jesus to Pilate to have him put to death is, as we have seen, a fact common to all the Gospels, and moreover appears at the earliest basis of the tradition. According to the accounts, this role is continued in the course of the audience: the high priests not only make the accusation against Jesus (Mark 15.3; Matt.27.12) but also spur on the crowd to call for his execution (Mark 15.11; Matt.27.20). The role of the Jewish crowd and its victory over the reluctant judge are an essential part of the four accounts, and can be removed only by turning one's back on history and seeing this feature solely as a symbol of the future Jewish hostility towards the growing church.

Certainly we could follow the theory of Jean Colin,[33] who

likens the judgment of Jesus to a vote by popular acclamation (*epiboêsis*), which was a constraint on the judge, similar to the practice in some cities, notably the free cities of the Greco-Roman East. However, this theory, which moreover is too inclined to take the accounts of the trial in the Gospels completely literally, suffers from several faults: it begins from too systematic an understanding of the practice in question; and it is wrong to apply the status of a free city to Judaea, where there is no attestation of such a practice. But, even if the crowd had no judicial power, would it not have come to the fore, from now on leaving the high priests on the sidelines, as the Gospels report? There are plenty of scenes in the history of the time, in particular under Pilate, in which we see the Jewish crowds intervening with the Roman authorities to make their desires known, sometimes extremely loudly.[34] In the circumstances it was all the easier for the high priests to stir up the people, brandishing a religious argument which presented Jesus as a blasphemous opponent of the temple, since the Passover pilgrimage attracted crowds to the sanctuary.[35]

However, one observation suggests that we should be cautious: the intervention of the crowd in the account of the first two Gospels is limited to the Barabbas episode. In Luke the crowd arrives much earlier (23.4), in connection with the high priest, by an anticipation which makes it possible to triple the single declaration of Jesus' innocence that we read in Mark (15.14).[36] For John, in this episode we have only the 'Jews' (19.7, 12, 14). The earliest version is to be found in Mark and Matthew, who bear witness to the separation of the two parts of the account in the tradition. Now the second, with the crowd's demand for the release of Barabbas, comes up against serious historical difficulties, as we shall see. That is why we can already express some doubt here about the vociferous throng in front of the governor's palace which the Gospels describe, and must suppose rather that a delegation from the Sanhedrin followed Jesus, surrounded by bodyguards, to notify Pilate of the reason for the arrest and to hand Jesus over to him. Probably all this happened without any popular tumult. Moreover such tumult would not have been to

Pilate's taste, and therefore would only have been an embarrassment for the accusers. The hierocrats, who were on the best terms
with the Romans and certainly were anxious not to compromise
their enterprise, had no interest in involving the crowd.

The place of the trial

In practice, the province of Judaea had two capitals. Caesarea
was the administrative capital where the Roman governor
usually resided. He sometimes went up to Jerusalem, particularly
on the occasion of the great Jewish festivals. The influx of people,
thronging there on pilgrimage, called for stricter supervision,
which was supported by the presence of the governor. That was
the situation at the time of the trial of Jesus.

Where the governor resided during his stays in Jerusalem is a
subject which is discussed particularly keenly: above all, or only,
because it was there that Jesus was judged and condemned. There
is no need to give a history of the debate here,[37] particularly as
today there are only two competing opinions: one opts for the
Antonia fortress, on the north-east angle of the temple forecourt,
and the other for Herod's palace, on the western hill of Jerusalem,
south-east of the present Jaffa gate. In fact the second location
seems far more likely. Since this question has been the object of
detailed studies,[38] I shall merely summarize the main arguments
in favour of this choice and refute some objections. First the
arguments:
– in Caesarea the governor's residence was Herod's palace, as we
are told by the Acts of the Apostles (23.35). Here we see Paul held
prisoner in 'the praetorium of Herod' by the procurator Felix. It is
inferred from this that Pilate similarly occupied the palace of the
old ruler in Jerusalem;
– the situation of Herod's palace, which dominated Jerusalem,
was ideal for keeping an eye on the whole city, and particularly on
the temple;
– in connection with the affair of the gilded shields, Philo clearly
identifies 'the governor's residence' with 'the palace of Herod';
– Josephus tells us that the procurator Gessius Florus lodged at

the 'palace' and that he had a rostrum constructed in front of it for giving audience to prominent people there;

– according to the Gospel of John (19.13), the place where Pilate sat to administer justice bore the Aramaic name *Gabbatha,* derived from the root *gb,* which in general evokes the idea of height or eminence.[39] The Antonia citadel indeed rose above the temple forecourt, but it could not claim to dominate the city, being even lower than the hill of Bezatha. The name certainly fits Herod's palace much better. The term used in Mark 15.8, which shows the crowd 'ascending' (*anabas*) to Pilate to ask pardon for Barabbas, points in the same direction. Whatever may be the historicity of the episode, in the first narrator this detail gives an idea of the local topography.

Two objections can be made to the location in Herod's palace: these relate, first, to the term 'praetorium', which in the Gospels denotes the edifice in question; then to the term *lithostroton,* the Greek rival of *Gabbatha* in John 19.13. In fact neither objection creates real difficulties. It is claimed that the word 'praetorium', far from necessitating the idea of a military building or barracks, had a broader sense and was used for 'the dwellings of ordinary local governors, not to mention any edifice destined to house the governor or other senior officials during their travels'.[40] As for the *lithostroton,* or 'paved area', while a pavement of large stones has been uncovered in the inner court of the Antonia, such pavements were by no means rare in the Graeco-Roman world, and an opponent of the location in Herod's palace recognized that 'the rare traces known today of the paving with which Herod Agrippa adorned the sreets of the city' show a pavement comparable to that of the Antonia.[41] Moreover the fact that a place in Jerusalem had a proper name in two forms, one of them in the local Aramaic, suggests that this was a public place used regularly rather than an enclosed space within a barracks reserved for the Roman army. The absence of any trace of paving in Herod's palace is regrettable, but does not give the lie to the positive arguments cited above.

So we should opt for Herod's palace as the framework for the Roman trial of Jesus: this was a real stronghold combined with a luxurious residence, of whose splendour Josephus boasts.[42] But we can perhaps be more precise. Mark (15.6) tells us that after being condemned and scourged, Jesus was taken by the soldiers 'within the palace,[43] which is the praetorium'. That presupposes that the previous events took place outside this same building. Certainly John contradicts this, for in his Gospel, apart from the end when Jesus is led 'out', all Pilate's dealings with the accused take place within the building, from which Pilate has to 'emerge' to meet 'the Jews'. However, the account is steeped in symbolism and by this coming and going indicates that from now on the Jews are deprived of revelation about the person of Jesus, the central theme of an 'interrogation' which is largely the construction of the evangelist. In describing a similar session, Josephus[44] confirms the location suggested by Mark: Jesus was judged and then scourged outside the palace, on the place called *Litho-stroton-Gabbatha*.

Pontius Pilate

Pontius Pilate was sent by Tiberius to succeed to Valerius Gratus as 'prefect'[45] of Judaea in 26 CE. It is difficult to be precise about his former existence. Since the post implies that he belonged to the equestrian order, Pilate will doubtless formerly have had a military career.[46] He spent ten years in Judaea, which he had to leave at the end of 36 or the beginning of the following year, when Vitellius, the legate of Syria, sent him to Rome to explain to Tiberius the massacre of the Samaritans of which he was accused.

The man does not deserve the merciless picture which Philo paints of him, nor the features of a weak-willed person yielding to the pressure of the crowd, as the Synoptic Gospels suggest.[47] His devoted submission to the emperor – the *Tiberium* in Caesarea is evidence of this – only partly explains the exceptional length of his time in Judaea, and we have to believe that he held office in a more than satisfactory way.[48] Nevertheless, he did so without much regard for the customs of the Jews, which he did not understand, and this led him to commit some blunders. On the other hand, we have every reason to accept that his relations with the local hierarchy were of the best: as we have already noted, Caiaphas remained high priest all the time that Pilate himself was in office, and when Pilate had to leave for Rome, Vitellius speedily nominated a successor to Caiaphas, a sign of connivance between Pilate and the latter.

As prefect of Judaea, Pilate was primarily a military leader (the sword he wore indicates this), responsible for maintaining public order, according to the principle enunciated by Cicero: 'Let the well-being of the [Roman] people be the supreme law.'[49] To this end Pilate and his like exercised a power of coercion which was limitless in the case of *peregrini* or those who were not Roman citizens. There was in fact no criminal code for these latter,[50] and the governors were free to fix their own rules. In practice, however, they tended to go by the *ordo* in force in Italy, and in procedure to take account of custom for want of any real legislation.

> Custom required that the judgment should be public, with the governor sitting on his dais or tribunal. The accusations had to be made in due form by the interested parties acting as private accusers (there was no public ministry in in the Roman world) and the accused had to have a chance to defend themselves. There were no juries, but normally a governor took the advice of a committee of assessors.[51]

Thus it was up to Jesus to make his own defence. We may presuppose the presence of an interpreter.[52]

The offences carrying the death penalty

Of what crime was Jesus accused before Pilate by the high priests? Neither Mark nor Matthew reports any details, far less John.[53] Luke (23.2) could hardly be more precise: 'We found this man perverting our nation, and forbidding us to give tribute to Caesar, and saying that he himself is Christ a king.' As I said earlier,[54] these are only the words of the author. However, here Luke's insight is correct, since he is developing something that Mark's account already suggests as a possibility and is confirmed by Matthew and John.

According to the four Gospels, Pilate's interrogation commences abruptly[55] with the question 'Are you the king of the Jews?' Doubtless this is the way in which the episode began in the source on which the evangelists depend. But the question presupposes prior information, the tenor of which it is not difficult to guess.

Some decades earlier, the political void created by the death of Herod the Great (4 BCE) had sparked off trouble. At that time, Josephus writes,[56] 'the whole of Judaea was rife with brigandry. Anyone could proclaim himself king at the head of a band of rebels to which he had attached himself to the detriment of the community, doing only insignificant damage to the Romans but causing the worst of slaughter among their own people'. Judas, son of Hezekiah, whose incursions Herod had repressed, was such a person: he sowed terror and exploited the country 'in his desire to increase his goods and in his ambition to obtain the royal dignity'.[57] Another brigand, by the name of Simon, a former slave of Herod, a giant of a man, put on the crown and was proclaimed king by his band, one of whose exploits was to pillage and burn the royal palace of Jericho.[58] Another Hercules who was also an indomitable character, Athronges or Athrongaios, a former shepherd, had four brothers, of the same stuff as himself:

> He put each of these in charge of an armed band, employing them as generals and satraps on his raids, and reserving to himself as king the settlement of major problems. He set a crown on his head, but continued for a considerable time to raid the country with his brothers. Their principal purpose was to kill Romans and the royal troops . . . [59]

At the beginning of the Jewish War (66), Menahem, a son of the famous rebel Judas of Gamala, called the Galilean, having seized Herod's palace, wanted to go to the temple, 'his head swollen he entered in pomp to worship, decked with kingly robes, and followed by a train of armed Zealots', before being assassinated by rival priests, perhaps because of his messianic claims.[60]

We should not doubt that the high priests handed Jesus over to Pilate presenting him in the guise of an agitator laying claim to the

throne. It is less certain that Pilate included in his interrogation
the direct question with which it begins in the Gospels. That is
certainly possible, above all if we see the question as being
scornfully ironical, but it could only have been remembered if
witnesses had heard it and then reported it in the first Christian
circles. As we have seen, the accounts of the session in the Gospels
have hardly any features which suggest a report from direct eye-
witnesses.[61] Similarly, it is probable that Pilate's question comes
from the placard about the condemned man which read 'king of
the Jews' (Mark 15.26), a public object the inscription of which
was easily retained in the popular memory.

The title thus exposed is a revealing one. It signifies that Jesus
was executed for having laid claim to royal power over his own
people. Such a claim was directly harmful to the Roman empire
and its rule. It fell under the accusation of *crimen maiestatis
populi romani* and, as such, carried the death penalty.[62]

Pilate was sufficiently impressed by the accusation to conclude
that it was necessary to pass the death sentence. At the least he
was taking a security measure, while wanting to satisfy a
hierocracy which was quite devoted to the Roman authorities.

If we now return to the reason for Jesus' arrest, accepting that it
was a criticism of the temple, we can see that the charge brought
before Pilate was a substantial modification of the one which had
set off the affair. However, that is not the view of K.Müller, who
begins from the role of the temple, which was both cultic and
political: since it had been the object of an attack by Jesus, it was
natural for Roman justice to intervene, as it intervened in the
affair of Jesus son of Ananias.[63] This theory is doubtful. There is
in fact nothing in this last example to indicate that Albinus agreed
to examine the case of Jesus son of Ananias in particular because
he was announcing misfortune relating to the temple. On the
other hand, everything combines to suggest that Pilate condemned Jesus for political pretensions to royalty. Now these pretensions, and the title 'king of the Jews' which sums up the charge
and the reason for the punishment inflicted, bear no relation to a
critical attitude towards the temple. As we have seen, the royal
pretenders who appeared among the Jews at this time were never

opposed to the sanctuary or its cult. Certainly the political impact of the temple and its system is undeniable, as is the hold the Romans had over its personnel.[64] But once again, if Jesus was condemned by Pilate for having spoken against the temple, the placard relating to the crucified Jesus will not have read 'the king of the Jews'.

However, let us note that the title does not oblige us to conclude that the high priests accused Jesus of having proclaimed himself king. To merit the title in question it was enough for him to have tried to seize power. That excludes any dynastic reference from the process. Whatever their information may have been, neither the high priests nor Pilate apparently showed the least belief or interest in Jesus' Davidic descent, unlike the Domitian of the legend who took umbrage at the descent of the grandsons of Jude, 'brother of the Lord'.[65]

Jesus before Herod Antipas?

In the Gospel of Luke, Pilate's interrogation is interrupted by an episode which shows Jesus being presented to Herod Antipas (Luke 23.6–12). The occasion for this is provided when Pilate learns that Jesus taught in Galilee, the tetrarchy of Antipas. The latter interrogates Jesus and, when he gets no reply, mocks him, as do his guards, and sends him back to Pilate: 'And Herod and Pilate became friends with each other that very day, for before this they had been at enmity with each other.'

Many contradictory opinions have been expressed about the origin and historicity of this account.[66] It is by no means improbable that Antipas was in Jerusalem for the Passover, and it is equally possible that Pilate, on his own initiative, wanted to take the tetrarch's advice.[67] Some arguments against the historicity of the episode are unconvincing, for example when it is seen as a fabrication intended to give historical substance to the quotation and the commentary on Ps.2.1–2 in Acts 4.25-27. In reality, the idea expressed in this last passage is precisely the opposite to what we read in the account of the passion since, instead of bearing witness in favour of Jesus (Luke 23.14–15),

'Herod and Pontius Pilate' are presented as his adversaries. It is hardly more appropriate to object that the attitude of Antipas during the trial contradicts the murderous plan imputed to him in Luke 13.31, since, far from seeming to come from a good traditional and historical source, this has all the appearance of being borrowed from Mark 6.14, artificially applying to Jesus what had formerly been said about John the Baptist.[68]

However, the other New Testament authors, and thus the tradition and the written sources which they had at their disposal, know nothing of the appearance before Herod, since one can hardly see what would have led them to omit it. In addition there are evident signs that this is a Lukan composition,[69] and it is embedded in a context from which it cannot be detached. The whole passage, text and context, is part of a plan which is not free of apologetic, since Herod supports Pilate's statement of innocence (Luke 23.15). These two voices, one Roman and the other Jewish, are paralleled in Acts when Agrippa II, another 'Jewish' king, agrees with the procurator Festus in recognizing that Paul has done nothing to merit the punishment of imperial justice (Acts 25.18, 25a; 26.31–32). For all these reasons it seems very difficult to detect the echo of a historical fact in the scene in question, even if we subtract the considerable role played by Luke here, and it would seem wise to exclude the tetrarch from those responsible for the death of Jesus.[70]

Barabbas

In the Gospel of Mark, the account of the Roman trial is divided into two distinct parts. In the first (15.2–5) we are present at a interrogation which stops abruptly; the crowd plays no role in it. The second part (15.6–15), in which the crowd intervenes actively, includes the Barabbas affair. This presentation is also that of Matthew (27.11–26), despite the additions I have mentioned.[71] Luke disturbs this structure by including the crowd in the accusation from the start (23.4).[72] The Barabbas episode exists in Luke only in an abbreviated form (23.18–19), without the slightest preparation and in a context (23.18–25) in which we can see no more than a recasting of Mark's narrative.[73] Here the Barabbas affair is secondary, as it is in John, who devotes only two verses to it (18.39–40). This diminution of interest in favour of other designs in the two evangelists does not dispense us from examining the Markan account, which attests the earliest form of the episode.

According to this Gospel, Pilate used to release a prisoner each Passover.[74] It is not said that another governor had done so. The crowd ascends to the palace to ask for the pardon in question. Pilate forestalls them and offers to free Jesus. The crowd refuses the offer and asks for the liberation of a certain Barabbas, whom we are told had been arrested with rebels[75] who had committed murder. We know what follows: Pilate finally accedes to the desires of the crowd.

The starting point here is the Passover amnesty, and the whole episode depends on its historicity. Now this custom is not attested anywhere outside the New Testament,[76] whether in connection with Pilate or in connection with some other governor of Judaea.

Josephus's silence on this point is an objection which is difficult to refute: as a friend of the Romans, would the historian have omitted something which related the clemency of those whose client he had become? Moreover all the analogies cited in support of the custom in question have only an extremely vague connection with it. The case drawn from the Mishnah is one of a prisoner freed provisionally by the *Jewish* authorities to allow him to celebrate the Passover.[77] We are even further from the circumstances evoked by the evangelist with the attempt to use as a comparison an expiatory ceremony, the first *lectisternium* celebrated at Rome, at which among other gestures of indulgence prisoners were freed from their chains and never had to put them on again.[78] The Florence Papyrus (61, 59f.)[79] reports the protocol of a trial before G.Septimius Vegetus, governor of Egypt in 85 CE: he freed a malefactor, a certain Phibion, at the request of the people. But this is a particular case, not a custom. There is no need to mention an even more remote recourse to the Babylonian calendars[80] to explain a Roman custom in Jerusalem in the first century of our era.

The fact remains that the proper name Barabbas (a Graeciza-tion of the Aramaic Bar Abba), well attested elsewhere,[81] bears the stamp of authenticity. We might add the introduction of this figure in Mark 15.7: Barabbas had been 'arrested with *the* rebels who had committed murder in *the* insurrection', a reference to a fact known to the first readers, at least at the level of the sources.[82] So it is probable that a rebel called Barabbas was freed by Pilate at the request of the crowd. Moreover this was not the only case in which the crowd thronged before the tribunal of the governor in Jerusalem.[83] We can even envisage that this took place the very day that Pilate condemned Jesus, as is suggested by the presence of others who were crucified in his company.[84] While we cannot know what led Pilate to release Barabbas, we can guess what led Mark and his predecessor to fuse the two events: by showing the crowd, urged on by the high priest, calling for the release of a murderer and the crucifixion of Jesus,[85] the report stigmatized the Jews for their iniquitous choice: at the same time it brought out the humanity of the Romans, which manifested itself in a regular act of clemency, confirmed by Pilate's reluctance to condemn Jesus.

Despite the way in which it is presented by the Gospels, the trial will have ended with a sentence pronounced in due form by Pilate from his rostrum.[86] From that moment, Jesus passed into the merciless hands of the troops.

6

Days and Hours

Here we touch on questions which have often been discussed and on which opinions differ considerably. We shall leave aside the problem of the year in which Jesus died, which in fact involves the whole of his public life,[1] and limit ourselves to the problems of the days and hours of his trial and execution.

The days

All the Gospels agree in fixing the death of Jesus on a Friday, the eve of the sabbath.[2] They differ in that according to the Synoptic Gospels, this Friday was the actual day of the Passover,[3] 15 Nisan, since Jesus and his disciples ate the Passover meal the previous night, whereas for John (18.28), this Friday was 14 Nisan, the eve of the Passover.

A learned attempt to harmonize the two chronologies has experienced some success in recent decades.[4] It stems from the discovery, in the book of Jubilees, of an ancient Jewish calendar based on the solar cycle, in which the festivals always fall on the same day of the week. This solar calendar was observed at Qumran, a place with links to the book of Jubilees. The Jerusalem temple followed the lunar calendar, in which the feasts are movable. Both calendars were current at the time of Jesus. Both fixed the Passover on 15 Nisan, but according to the former the 15 Nisan always fell on a Tuesday, whereas according to the latter it could fall on any day of the week. Jesus will have followed the former calendar and celebrated the Passover on the night of Monday/Tuesday, which extends the events of the passion from

Tuesday to Friday, much longer than appears from the Gospels. Since the high priests observed the other calendar, we can understand why John 18.28 reports that they did not enter the praetorium so as not to defile themselves and so that they could eat the Passover. Several ancient writings (the Syriac Didascalia, Epiphanius, Victorinus of Pettau, the Book of Adam and Eve) fall in with this theory by stating formally that Jesus ate the Passover on Tuesday evening.

This solution comes up against too many difficulties to be acceptable.[5] Right at the beginning and well before the composition of the Gospels, Paul reports the *tradition* which puts the last meal of Jesus with his disciples on 'the night when he was delivered up' (I Cor.11.23). And the patristic evidence in favour of Tuesday most certainly derives from a concern to provide a basis for the Wednesday and Friday fasts. Moreover it is in no way inconceivable that the facts of the passion reported by the Gospels should have taken place in the time assigned to them, whereas we do not know how to fill the void extending from Jesus' Passover to his arrest. Why, one could add, should Jesus have adopted a 'sectarian'-type calendar, when he has no links with any dissidents and everything leads us to believe that he remained within mainstream Judaism in order to propagate his message and his reform there? Finally, we may ask how Jesus could have obtained a lamb which had been properly slaughtered at the temple, an indispensable condition for celebrating the festival. This objection can hardly be met by imagining, quite gratuitously, a place in the temple reserved for Essenes to slaughter the lambs on their date;[6] nor is it any improvement to think of lambs being slaughtered in the houses where the Passover was eaten or, as after the destruction of the temple, a Passover without a lamb: this is sheer fantasy, with no foundation in the texts.

Recourse to astronomy proves disappointing in trying to resolve the difference between the Synoptics and the Fourth Gospel, which we cannot avoid doing.[7] On the other hand, there are several possible arguments of another order which shift the balance towards the Synoptic side.

The main argument in favour of the Synoptics is that historic-
ally the last meal of Jesus with his disciples was a Passover meal.
Everything is linked with this, and Jesus .was crucified on 15
Nisan, the day of the Passover.

To establish that the meal in question really was the Passover
meal and that it does not owe its Passover character to primitive
Christianity, we can make several observations linked both to
New Testament texts and to contemporary Jewish usages.[8] Here
are just some of the essential arguments and a refutation of the
main objections.

First of all, according to all four Gospels, Jesus' last meal took
place in Jerusalem. This was the rule after the lambs had been
slaughtered on the temple forecourt. According to the Gospel
tradition, confirmed by Paul (I Cor.11.23), the meal took place by
night. Now nocturnal meals were not customary among the Jews,
who took their main meal around sunset, except for Passover,
when the later time was an obligation.[9]

Granted, the reference to the Passover does not appear in the
accounts of the institution of the eucharist in the New Testament.
But these are ritual texts describing a practice from then on
repeated throughout the year by Christians, unlike the Jewish
Passover, which was annual.

Another objection is derived from the note in Mark 15.21,
which mentions Simon of Cyrene 'coming in from the country'
when Jesus is on his way to the place of execution. Doesn't this
indicate an infringement of the rule that people must rest on the
day of Passover? But even supposing that Simon was a Jew, and
thus obliged to rest at Passover, first the text does not say that he
was returning from work in the country.[10] As for the distance
covered, it does not necessary need to be more than the 880
metres, measured from the inhabited part of the town, which was
the authorized distance that could be travelled. Moreover, if we
take account of its Semitic parallels, the expression *ap'agrou* may
well simply mean 'outside the city', without being any more
precise.[11]

But doesn't John's chronology find an ally in Mark himself? At
the beginning of the passion narrative, John tells us that the

Jewish authorities mean to engage in their murderous enterprise against Jesus outside the 'feast' (Mark 14.2). Isn't this notice a vestige of tradition which confirms the Johannine presentation against Mark? Some scholars think so. But in reality a precise study of Mark 14.1–2 sees it as a creation of the evangelist from beginning to end, and the contradiction perceived between this passage and what follows (14.12, 14, 16) is easy to resolve if, with a large number of scholars,[12] we accept that the word *heortê* in Mark 14.2 has the local sense of 'festal crowd'. Moreover this sense, which has some support outside Mark, is the only one that fits in with the plan of the authorities to act 'by stealth' *(en doloi:* Mark 14.1);[13] it also matches the nature of the operations which are described later: everything goes on at night, shielded from the view of the population.

Finally, it might seem surprising that a crucifixion took place on the day of the Passover. But this was the work of the Roman soldiers, who were indifferent to Jewish worship. Moreover, 'the presence of the crowds at the feast may have seemed to the Romans to provide an opportunity for using the three executions as an impressive deterrent'.[14]

However, we still have to take account of the different chronology of the Fourth Gospel.

One fact is obvious: Jesus emphatically brings out the Passover framework of the death of Jesus. Once announced (John 11.55; 12.1), the theme is solemnly brought to the fore at the beginning of the last phase of the Gospel (13.1). Three times, as a leitmotiv, the Passover is mentioned in the passion narrative (18.28, 39; 19.14). But there is also the fact that in John 1.29,36 Jesus is designated the 'lamb of God'. This is a mysterious title, which probably had many connotations, and we cannot exclude an allusion to the Passover lamb, all the more so since this typological relationship is attested elsewhere in the New Testament (I Cor.5.7; I Peter 1.19).[15] We might add the scriptural quotation in John 19.36: 'Not a bone of him shall be broken'. Though this quotation cannot be identified word for word in the Bible, it too refers to the Paschal lamb.[16] Although the evangelist does not reveal his intentions in making Jesus die at the moment when the lambs were being killed at the temple for the paschal meal, the evidence we have just gathered from him hardly allows any doubt: for John, if Jesus dies on the eve of the Passover and not the day after, as he does according to the Synoptics, this is so that his death can coincide with the 'Passover of the Jews',[17] and so that it can be seen that henceforth he is a substitute for it (John 1.17). To anyone who knows Johannine thought and method this will seem to be the best solution of this old problem.[18]

The hours

John and the Synoptic Gospels also disagree over the hours as well as the days. According to Mark (15.25), Jesus was crucified at the 'third hour', nine in the morning; at the sixth hour (noon) he is still on the cross (15.33), as he is at the ninth hour, three o'clock in the afternoon (15.34). The last two indications are reproduced in Matthew (27.45,46) and Luke (23.44). John (19.14), however, puts the end of the session before Pilate 'around the sixth hour', towards noon. These two timetables are radically incompatible, and attempts to resolve the contradiction[19] are sheer fancy. But are these precise details, aimed at informing the reader of the real course of events? The practice of the Gospels allows us to suspect other intentions.

In Mark the timetable involves intervals of three hours. This schematism cannot be explained, as some scholars attempt,[20] by resorting to the 'chronological determinism' of the apocalypses, since these do not offer any parallels to the mention of the hours in the form it takes in Mark, and despite the darkness (15.33), the context of the Gospel falls outside the apocalyptic genre. Another explanation has been proposed: the timetable of the passion is aligned on the daily prayer of Christians.[21] Prayer three times a day, not in conformity to contemporary Jewish usage,[22] but inspired by the Old Testament (Ps.55.18; Deut.6.11), is prescribed in the Didache (8.3). The Acts of the Apostles puts prayers at the sixth (10.9) and ninth hours (3.1; 10.30), thus paralleling two-thirds of the timetable of the Markan passion.[23] If we cannot assert that in his redaction Mark had the hours of Christian prayer in view, the contacts which I have just indicated at least make this plausible. The fact remains that at all events this timetable is artificial and, for want of any other aim, helps the reader to divide up this memorable day between the 'morning' when Jesus is handed over to Pilate (15.1) and the 'evening' of his burial (15.42).

If that is the case, the Markan timetable of the passion leaves the historian uncertain. The same is certainly true of the timetable of the Fourth Gospel, but not for the same reason. Did the evangelist use (and correct) Mark, or does he depend on another source (which on this point is historical)? John had to get Jesus to Calvary after noon, since that was when the lambs were killed in the temple, according to the typology the indications of which were collected together above.

We can conclude that Jesus was executed during the day of 15 Nisan, the day of the Passover. The session of the tribunal presided over by Pilate will have taken place early in the morning, not only because of the precise detail given in Mark 15.1 but also because that corresponds to Roman custom, in which public life began at daybreak.[24] The indications in the Gospel do not allow us to draw any certain conclusions about the precise hour of the crucifixion.

7

The Execution

The troops[1] stationed in the provinces administered by a prefect, and under his orders, were auxiliaries. Unlike legions composed of Roman citizens, these units were made up of provincials who had no citizenship rights. In Judaea they were recruited mainly from among the non-Jewish inhabitants of Palestine, since the Jews were exempt from service in the Roman army. The soldiers to whom Jesus was handed over after being condemned were either those occupying the Antonia[2] or the militia which had accompanied Pilate from Caesarea. One or other of these were responsible for inflicting a first punishment, as a prelude to crucifixion.

The scourging

The evangelists are extremely discreet over the memory of the scourging of Jesus. One word – in the first three Gospels a simple participle – expresses it. Mark (15.15) and Matthew (27.26) mention the fact itself. In Luke (23.14,22) the scourging is only announced as Pilate's intention, without any mention of its being inflicted, and in this connection the evangelists use a euphemism (*paideuein*, 'educate', but also 'chastize'); moreover, here the scourging appears as an independent punishment aimed at satisfying the accusers. John (19.1–2) behaves similarly by making the scourging (followed by a scene of derision) an episode within the Roman trial, for the purpose of preparing for the *Ecce homo* and a new confrontation with the Jews.

The reality was certainly different. Though rendered better in the version of Mark and Matthew, the sequence of events is hardly identified as clearly as one could have wished. But any reading is superficial and erroneous which deduces from the text of the Gospels that the scourging preceded the death sentence, as an independent punishment.[3] In reality, the texts in question, as I demonstrated earlier,[4] do not mention any sentence. The scourging was the prelude to crucifixion.

That is in fact how things usually happened: those condemned to the cross were first flogged.[5]

The evangelists other than Luke use two so to speak technical terms to denote this punishment: Mark and Matthew have the Latinism *phragelloun*, John has *mastigoun*; there seems no clear way of distinguishing these verbs. According to Sherwin-White,[6] the Roman jurists established a progression in this kind of punishment extending from the mildest to the most severe, described by three terms: *fustes, flagella, verbera*. However, in reality[7] neither the New Testament nor the Roman legal sources make a clear distinction between the two latter forms, in terms either of their role or of their severity. Moreover we do not even know for what precise purpose these punishments in their various forms were administered: as a warning, as torture to obtain a confession, or as a prelude to crucifixion and therefore as an integral part of capital punishment.

This last case applies to Jesus. A victim of this barbarous punishment,[8] he was doubtless treated just like the others. If he did not collapse under the blows – which was quite frequent – this was above all because the following act involved the crucifixion of a living body, not a corpse. In any case, anyone who survived the whips of the executioners was only a shred of humanity.

Jesus was flogged in public. What we can deduce from Mark 15.16[9] is confirmed by the account, already mentioned, of the savage repression of an insurrection by the procurator Gessius Florus (64–66) on the eve of the Jewish war: when the revolt was put down, it was 'before the rostrum' (*pro tou bematos*) set up 'in front of the palace' that Florus had Jews of equestrian rank, Roman citizens, first scourged and then crucified.[10] The same thing happened to Jesus, who suffered the first stage of his punishment at the place called *lithostroton* or *Gabbatha*,[11] where he had just been judged and condemned.

Derision

Mark (15.16–20) and Matthew (27.27–31) have the session of Pilate's tribunal followed by a scene in which we see Jesus ridiculed and maltreated by the soldiers. Luke has nothing of the kind at this point: we know that he deliberately omits anything that insults the dignity of Jesus too much. As has been pointed out, John includes this scene artificially in the body of the appearance before Pilate (19.1–3).

In Mark's description we can note an element which has probably come from elsewhere: the scene is framed by acts of violence which break up its overall unity (15.19) and which recall the insults suffered by Jesus from the servants of the high priest (Mark 14.65).[12] Without this supplement the scene is a perfect unity: stripped and then reclothed in his garments (which prepares for their being divided at Calvary), Jesus is meanwhile disguised as a vassal king: with a red cloak,[13] a crown hastily made from a thorny shrub, and a reed in his hand as a sceptre, he presented a parody for the homage of the soldiers. They invited others[14] to enjoy the spectacle and join in the mockery.

But is the scene historical? Certainly it is hard to imagine a Christian writer enjoying inventing such a degrading position for Jesus, who moreover is the victim of the Roman soldiers, contrary to the general tendency of the Gospels to give the Romans the better role in the account of the passion. Moreover the fact that Jesus was mocked for his pseudo-royalty fits the charge to which the inscription over the condemned man bears witness (Mark 15.26 par.).[15] But we should also note some difficulties which raise doubts as to the reality of the facts.

The least objection is that the scene has a counterpart earlier (Mark 14.65 par.; Matt.26.67–68) and that the two passages structure the account of the passion after each session of the tribunal. However, the schematic nature of the whole passage is not enough reason to declare the second account to have no historical basis: the narrator could have used a recollection, all the more since the facts related in the two cases do not coincide. Two other objections are harder to refute. One is that this carnival-like enthronement is said to have taken place within the palace (Mark 15.16 par. Matt.27.27), so that there would have been no witness capable of passing it on to the first Christian communities. The second notes that the scene is only partially original.

This last comment is fair, though certain parallels have been adduced to conclude that here we have a simple phenomenon of literary imitation. The Persian festival of the Sacaea and the Saturnalia offer only a distant resemblance.[16] We have something closer when we read Philo's account of the caricature of Agrippa I,[17] lampooned in Alexandria by mimes and other buffooneries of this kind:

> There was a certain lunatic named Carabas . . . He spent day and night in the streets naked, shunning neither heat nor cold, made game of by the children and the lads who were idling about. The rioters drove the poor fellow into the gymnasium and set him up on high to be seen of all, and put on his head a sheet of byblus spread out wide for a diadem, clothed the rest of his body with a rug for a royal robe, while someone who had noticed a piece of the native papyrus thrown away on the road gave it to him for his sceptre. And when as in some theatrical game he had received the insignia of kingship and had been tricked out as a king, young men carrying rods on their shoulders as spearmen stood on either side of him in imitation of a bodyguard. Then others advanced on him, some pretending to salute him, others to sue for justice, others to consult him on state affairs. Then from the multitudes standing around him there rang out a tremendous shout, hailing him as *Marin*, which is the name for 'lord' in Syria. For they knew that Agrippa was both a Syrian by birth and had a great piece of Syria over which he was king.[18]

While there is no point in imagining any dependence of the Christian narrator on Philo, this anecdote could have circulated in Palestinian circles, despite the good will with which the Jews later surrounded their ephemeral sovereign because of his ostentatious piety. There are many common features in the cruel farce and that described by the Gospels: false crown[19] and gimcrack sceptre made of plants, a makeshift royal cloak, the burlesque homage of those standing by including the royal title, all details which, with the necessary adaptations, could have inspired the author of the first account of the passion. However, it is not necessary to accept that everything was invented. Even without direct witnesses the rumour could have spread that Jesus had been spat on and ridiculed by the soldiers, and it was easy to pad this out, making use of the still-recent recollection[20] of the fate inflicted on the poor madman of Alexandria.

Towards Calvary

Contrary to the impression created by Luke (23.25–26) and John (19.16), it was not the Jews but the Roman soldiers who led Jesus to the place of execution. A number of examples attest that the condemned man himself carried the instrument of his execution, in this case the cross-beam (*patibulum*), which subsequently had to be raised to the post fixed into the ground (*stipes crucis*); this was the case despite the expression 'bear one's cross'.[21]

Apart from the Fourth Evangelist (19.17) in his concern to mark the voluntary and sovereign character of the act, the witnesses are unanimous in saying that the soldiers requisitioned a passer-by, a certain Simon who was coming into the city, to carry Jesus' cross. This suggests that Jesus had carried it himself at least for some paces.[22] It also indicates that Jesus was too weak to carry it after enduring the scourging. The reality of the fact is confirmed by the details given about the person who was conscripted for this task.

This Simon came from Cyrene, capital of the North African region of Cyrenaica. A number of Jews lived there.[23] Some of them who had settled in Jerusalem had a synagogue in the city.[24] Rather than being a pilgrim who had come for the festival, Simon was a member of this community. For by indicating the name of his sons, Alexander and Rufus,[25] the tradition which had come down to Mark indicated that these were individuals known to the Christians of Jerusalem. That leads us to conclude that the family, living in the Holy City, joined the disciples of the crucified Jesus. A tomb cut in the rock was discovered in 1941, in the place called Karm esh-Sheikh, south-east of the Kidron valley. It contained eleven ossuaries, one of which bore among other inscriptions, 'Alexander [son] of Simon', with an addition (*qrnyt*). A correction to *qrnyh* would make it possible to identify this as the place where the family of the man who carried Jesus' cross were buried.

fig. 16.

ΑΛΕΞΑΝΔΡΟΥ	*of Alexander*
אלכסנדרוס קרנית	*Alexander QRNYT*

From N.Avigad, 'A Depository of Inscribed Ossuaries in the Kidron Valley', *Israel Exploration Journal* 12, 1962, 10.

Here we can only make careful conjectures.[26] At all events, given its origin – which could confirm the foreign names of Simon's two sons[27] – this family could have been part of the Hellenistic group of the Christian community in Jerusalem at whose autonomy and mixed fortunes Acts allows us to guess. Should we suppose that some members of this family were among the innovators who preached the gospel to the Greeks of Antioch (Acts 11.20 includes Cyreneans among them)? Be this as it may, only in imagination can we trace the course which began with a chance encounter with the man on the way to execution and ended in belief in his person.[28]

The pitiful picture of a Jesus at the end of his strength, led by the soldiers, is hardly compatible with the station of the cross described in Luke 23.27–31. Moreover the presence of a cortège of weeping women presents additional difficulties. The funeral lamentations took place after death, at the time of burial.[29] Furthermore, these demonstrations were forbidden in the case of executed criminals.[30] Whatever may be the origin of this episode, it is the framework of an oracle which expresses, after the event and with the help of scriptural reminiscence, the Christian reading of the capture of Jerusalem by the Romans in 70.

It remains for us to identify the route taken by Jesus to the place of execution. Since the residence of the governor where Jesus was condemned and scourged has now been identified with Herod's palace on the western hill of Jerusalem,[31] we must next determine the site of Golgotha.

This word, recorded by all the evangelists apart from Luke,[32] is the approximate Greek transcription of the Aramaic *gulgulta* (Hebrew *gulgolet*) which means 'skull' (in Latin *Calvaria*, hence 'Calvary'). This name, given without explanation, has not entirely yielded up its secret. However, if we dismiss as improbable the idea that skulls could be found scattered at this place,[33] the only possible consideration is its topographical configuration. Certainly the evangelists never speak of a hill or a hillock at this place, and we cannot draw any conclusions from the present position of 'Golgotha' in the Holy Sepulchre, at a height of 4.92 metres from the ground: the changes in the terrain over history prevent us from arriving at assured conclusions. But the Pilgrim of Bordeaux, who visited Jerusalem in 333, claimed to have seen a *monticulus Golgotha*.[34] Without attaching absolute value to reports which are more dominated by piety than archaeological perspicacity, we can hardly go wrong in accepting that 'this name was given to a rounded rocky hillock . . . because it stood out, just as today people use the term *ras* (head) for certain natural excrescences which have no resemblance whatever to anything human'.[35] The need to give the execution a public character points in the same direction.

All these places vanished from sight as a result of the

transformations of the area through the embankments constructed on the orders of the emperor Hadrian when in 135 Jerusalem became Aelia Capitolina. However, it is significant that before the building of the Constantinian basilica the more ancient pilgrims,[36] who could on longer see the places in question since they were at that time covered by pagan buildings, never speak of any veneration of them by Christians. They indicate that no one ever dared to produce a false Golgotha or a false Holy Sepulchre[37] for the needs of piety, and therefore that they knew where the supposedly authentic places were. Then, when the first basilica was constructed on the orders of Constantine, enormous clearance work was needed[38] in a place which must have made architects shudder, proof that this was the place indicated by tradition.

But how valid is this tradition, which is firmly anchored in the third and fourth centuries? The answer is for archaeology,[39] in other words for excavations, to give. Unfortunately these have never been made methodically because of the buildings which cover the site of the Holy Sepulchre. Moreover the debate on the question of the place of Calvary and the tomb of Jesus, and the doubts surrounding it, depend on another controversial point. This concerns the 'second wall' of Jerusalem, built either by a Hasmonaean king or by Herod to protect the north of the city, and described by Josephus.[40] One of the main recent objections to the traditional site was that this rampart enclosed it, which would put the place of Jesus' execution within the city, contrary to the New Testament and above all to the Jewish law and Roman custom.[41] In fact at that time the traces of the wall had more or less been identified with the present rampart. Vincent passionately tried to re-establish what he thought to be the truth by presenting a detailed description of the supposed remains of the second wall, on the basis of excavations made in the Mauristan district. Vincent's plan, which has often been reproduced and has become classic, is now obsolete. Thanks to more recent excavations made in the same area by Kathleen Kenyon and Ute Lux, on the occasion of the restoration of the Lutheran Church of the Redeemer, it seems quite clear that the wall, the most important

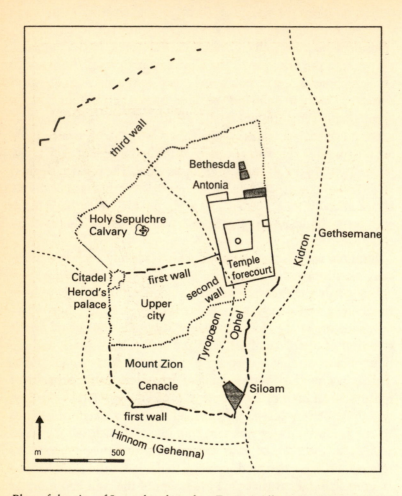

Plan of the city of Jerusalem based on Eugeno Alliata, *La Terre sainte* 2, March–April 1992, 80. Note the line of the first wall and the vague location of the second and third walls. A dotted line indicates the limits of the city today.

Reconstruction of the Mauristan quarter before 70 CE.

Sketch by E.Sawadsky, from B.E.Schein, 'The Second Wall of Jerusalem', *Biblical Archaeologist* 44, 1981, 24.

part of which crosses the centre of the church, is a construction dating from the late empire and cannot be seen as the second wall spoken of by Josephus. At present it is impossible to determine the contours of this rampart, except to make it end at the Antonia, again according to the indications of Josephus.[42] However, archaeologists conclude that its traces do not compromise the authenticity of the traditional sites, since at all events it already passed within the area in question.[43] The discovery in 1885 of some first-century tombs near to the basilica of the Holy Sepulchre (one of them wrongly called the 'tomb of Joseph of Arimathea') offers confirmation here, given that it was both the Jewish and the Roman rule to bury the dead outside the cities.

We can only guess at the actual site of Golgotha. A vast quarry extended under the greater part of the basilica and its southern courtyard. It ceased to be worked towards the south-east at a rocky spur rising on its western and northern faces to a height of around five metres.[44] Are we to see this as the actual place of crucifixion? Archaeologists remain cautious here.

The Fourth Gospel (19.41) puts a 'garden' (*kêpos*) 'at the place where Jesus had been crucified' and where he had been buried. This garden evokes the 'Garden Gate' situated not far from there. Arguing from the reticence in rabbinic literature about the planting of fruit trees near to a burial ground, R.E.Brown[45] suggests that this 'garden' originates in the literary necessity to prepare for the mistake made by Mary of Magdala in confusing Jesus with the 'gardener' (*kêpouros,* John 20.15). That is unconvincing; it is much more probable that John is giving us good topographical information and that in fact the quarry had been 'converted into a "garden", i.e. cultivable ground, of which other examples exist today, particularly around Bethlehem. Large chunks of red earth were brought in, and excavations have come upon the remains of them mixed up with stone chippings in the hollows of the quarry.'[46]

Though we cannot identify with sufficient certainty a specific site for the execution of Jesus, we can say that to within a few metres the site of Golgotha lay, in a straight line, around 400 metres from Herod's palace or the praetorium. Now we can only say that Jesus must have followed a route created to impress the population, since that was ancient practice.[47] We cannot say by which gate of the city he left by and how, whether this was the Yeshana Gate (or Gate of Ephraim) or the Gennath Gate (Garden Gate),[48] one 80 metres and the other 250 metres from the traditional Golgotha. We also need to note that there is no serious archaeological evidence to support the Via Dolorosa which pilgrims continue to follow today and which begins from the site of the Antonia.

The crucifixion and death of Jesus

The last moments of Jesus are related in the Gospels for the purpose of religious instruction and edification which governs all the accounts of the passion. The maximum number of appeals for readers to reflect, which for the most part are drawn from the Old Testament and are aimed at establishing a harmony between these cruel facts and the words of the holy books, are concentrated in the few verses in Mark[49] and the other Synoptic Gospels, to which the Fourth Gospel is to be added. Luke combines with this a particular concern to bring out the example offered by Jesus to Christians at this supreme moment. The task of the historian consists in stripping these accounts of their embellishments, in order as far as possible to discover the original facts.[50]

The narcotic

According to Mark (15.23,36) and Matthew (27.34,48), Jesus is twice given something to drink on Calvary. The first time, before the crucifixion, Mark writes that this was 'wine mingled with myrrh' (*esmyrnismenon*, literally 'myrrhed'). We shall keep to this version in preference to that of Matthew, who speaks of 'wine mingled with gall', an adaptation inherited from Ps.69 (LXX 86).22. In Mark the mixture is a narcotic.[51] This humanitarian gesture corresponds to a Jewish,[52] not a Roman custom; so, despite the evangelists, who make the soldiers the

ones who offer it, we should think of Jewish men or women here.
The tradition will not have retained something which was to the
advantage of the Jews, preferring to credit it to the Romans. A
witness to the scene may have remembered that Jesus refused the
narcotic, as Mark reports.[53] But this is above all an additional
illustration of Jesus' mastery in the face of suffering.[54]

The crucifixion

The crucifixion of Jesus is mentioned in the four Gospels without
the slightest detail, even in passing, about the one who endured
this form of execution.[55] On this point the evangelists felt a
horror and disgust which partly escape us today after twenty
centuries of having grown accustomed to it, but which they
shared with their contemporaries. In fact the witnesses of the
imperial period are unanimous in regarding this punishment as
the most cruel and degrading of all – that is why it was
traditionally reserved for the lower classes of society.[56]

Practised by the Romans and regarded as a typically Roman
punishment, crucifixion was nevertheless used occasionally by
the Greeks[57] and the Jews themselves. Around 88 BCE Alexander Jannaeus had eight hundred rebels who had been taken
prisoner crucified right in the middle of Jerusalem.[58] This affair is
recalled in the Nahum Commentary discovered at Qumran
(4QpNahum 2,6–8). This document leaves no doubt about the
form of execution: it was crucifixion and not the suspension of
the bodies of the executed men after they had been put to death,
as Deuteronomy (21.22–23) prescribes. Another text from
Qumran, the Temple Scroll (11QTemple 64,6–13), does not
mention the misdeeds of Alexander Jannaeus but describes the
punishment of two kinds of offenders: those guilty of high
treason and offenders absconding before trial. If we use the first
text to interpret the second, leaving out later rabbinic texts, it
would seem that the Essene milieu envisaged crucifixion (and not
strangulation by hanging) as a punishment for certain crimes.[59]
However, we cannot say whether this legislation was other
than theoretical, since we have no instance to confirm its

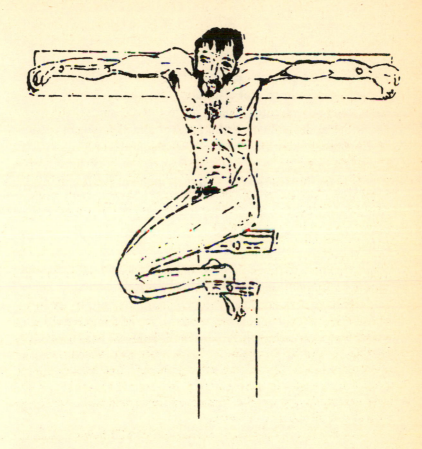

Sketch based on the remains of the crucified man discovered at Giv'at ha-Mivtar, Jerusalem (*Le Monde de la Bible* 2, 1978, 43).

application.[60] Josephus for his part does not mention any case of crucifixion under Herod. It was not long before the systematic Roman custom was applied: on the death of the monarch and to repress the revolt which followed, in 4 BCE Varus had 2,000 rebels crucified in Jerusalem.[61] With the direct government of Judaea by Rome, crucifixion became established in this province, as is shown by the case of Jesus and numerous others.

How Jesus was executed is not easy to retrace, since there were various forms, depending on the fantasy and the sadism of the executioners. In reporting the massive crucifixion (up to 500 a day) of Jewish fugitives by Titus during the siege of Jerusalem, Josephus notes that 'the soldiers, in their anger and out of hatred, ridiculed the prisoners by nailing them each in a different posture'.[62] The executioners of Jesus doubtless had less reason to resort to such refinements, but it is still distressing to describe in detail the procedure that they used.

At all events, we can be certain that the condemned man was stripped of his clothing and crucified entirely naked.[63] Jesus would not have been an exception here, and it is hard to see how in the event the Roman soldiers would have had any regard for the Jewish modesty which is evident in the rules in the Mishnah.[64] Only the Gospel of Nicodemus[65] gives Jesus the privilege of a loincloth.

It is quite evident how Jesus was fixed to the cross: he was nailed to it,[66] not attached. The prime evidence of this comes from the New Testament writings. Already when Luke (24.39–40) reports that the risen Jesus showed his hands and his feet to his disciples, it is clear that they were thought of as bearing scars. But John (20.25–27) is explicit in drawing attention to the 'marks of the nails' (*ho typos tôn hêlôn*) in the hands. To that can be added all the mentions of the blood of Jesus in the New Testament, blood which was indubitably shed on the cross and not during the scourging.[67] Among other external evidence in confirmation we might cite Josephus, who on occasion uses the expression 'nail [*proseloun*][to the cross]' for 'crucify', and attests that crucifixion involved bloodshed.[68]

The valuable discovery of the skeleton of a crucified man

named Yehohanan in 1968 in the Giv'at ha-Mivtar district of Jerusalem confirms the fact, indirectly indicated in Luke 24.39–40 and later accepted by Justin, that Jesus' feet were also nailed.[69] Plautus gives an example to the same effect when, in the *Mostellaria,* he makes the slave Tranio, evoking an exceptionally cruel form of execution, say: 'I will give a talent to the first who will ascend the cross [in my place], but on condition that his feet and his arms are nailed twice.'[70] This text offers a detail confirming the exhumation mentioned above, which shows a wound in the forearm, and not in the two hands. That supports the medical opinions which doubt the possibility of suspending a body with nails put in the palms, above all without any support. Thus to put Jesus' wounds in the forearm does not contradict the facts of the Gospels, which speak of 'hands'; this term could be extended. Are we to envisage one or two nails for the feet?[71] While granting the executioners a reasonable degree of freedom in performing their task, we may note that the feet of the crucified man of Giv'at ha-Mivtar were fixed to the cross by one nail through the heel-bone. The *sedile*, a block put in the middle of the upright to support the body, is only mentioned later in texts,[72] but it seems to have been necessary to prevent the corpse from slumping and bringing about a rapid death, contrary to the intended aim, namely to make the cross 'a slow punishment'.[73] The support for the feet (*hypopodion, suppedaneum*) does not appear before the first half of the third century.[74] Jesus was nailed to the cross lying down, his arms stretched out on the crossbeam, which was then hoisted with the body on to the stake which had already been fixed into the ground.[75] From the fact that, according to Mark 15.36, to give a drink to the crucified Jesus it was necessary to use a sponge on the end of a reed, we may suppose a relatively high cross – which was not always the case – with Jesus' feet around a metre above the ground.[76]

The companions in the execution

According to the four Gospels,[77] two other condemned men were crucified with Jesus. Luke makes the most of this with the episode

of the 'penitent thief' (23.39–43). This evangelist emphasizes
more than the others the association with Jesus in his execution of
men whom he describes with the generic and strictly moral term
'malefactors' (*kakourgoi*) (23.32, 33, 39); here it is a matter of
affirming the fulfilment of the scriptures (Isa.53.12, cited in Luke
22.37). By emphasizing that Jesus was crucified between his two
companions in misfortune – 'one on the right hand, the other on
the left' according to the Synoptic Gospels, and 'one on each side,
with Jesus in the centre' according to John – the texts produce a
pictorial effect which can only be deliberate. However, it is hard
to know how to challenge the basic reality of this note.
Immediately exploited by the first Christian narrators, it hardly
moves in a direction which is accentuated from one Gospel to
another, since by being associated with other condemned men,
Jesus loses an isolation which would make him stand out. So here
we have the recollection of a collective execution[78] in which Jesus
was included, the number 'three' also being suspect by reason of
its schematism.

In Mark (15.27) and Matthew (27.38), his companions are
described as *leistai,* 'brigands'. Here we must guard against the
influence of reading Flavius Josephus, who uses this term to
denote rebels, especially those engaged in the revolt against the
Romans.[79] As such, and in Josephus himself, the term has less
specific meanings, among other things denoting ordinary thieves
or highwaymen.[80] So there is no need to see the others executed
on Calvary as rebels, extending to them the accusation made
against Jesus. It sufficed that they disturbed public order enough
to merit the supreme punishment.

Dividing the garments

Among the features which make up the scene on Calvary, the
sharing of Jesus' garments by lot is mentioned in the four Gospels.
However, John (19.23–24) is more specific about the operation:
the execution squad, composed of four soldiers, take the outer
garments,[81] dividing them into four; when they get to the tunic
(*chitōn,* the long shirt worn next to the skin), the soldiers draw

lots for it, since it was in one piece without a seam. The custom of assigning the personal effects of those executed to their executioners was legalized among the Romans,[82] so it is natural that this detail should have been reported in the case of Jesus. The drawing of lots, in which we recognize the very words of Ps.22 (LXX 21).19 (explicitly quoted in John 19.24), is far less certain. A concern for verisimilitude has guided the pen of the Fourth Gospel in producing the detail of the indivisible tunic,[83] thus justifying the procedure in question.

The placard

Mark (15.26) tells us of the 'inscription' (*epigraphe*) which gave the reason for the condemnation of Jesus, who was thus labelled 'the king of the Jews'. According to Matthew (27.37) the phrase was 'This is the king of the Jews', and the inscription was fixed to the cross above Jesus' head. Luke (23.38) gives the same information as Matthew, but more briefly. The Fourth Gospel is far more eloquent here (John 19.19–22). Pilate himself is said to have produced a 'placard' (*titlos*, from the Latin *titulus*), which bore in Hebrew, Greek and Latin the words 'Jesus of Nazareth, king of the Jews', and to have had it put on the cross. The emphasis and the abundance of this last testimony strongly recalls the thought and theology of the evangelists, and one doubts whether Pilate would have made so much of a man condemned to the cross. As for the trilingual text, although the epigraphy of tombs and official documents from antiquity attest this sort of thing,[84] we can see it above all as the proclamation of the kingship of Jesus to the whole world.

Neither Matthew nor Luke were present at the crucifixion of Jesus, nor was Mark, but on occasion he nevertheless reports recollections coming from eye-witnesses. We cannot doubt that the detail of the placard derives from the experience of these latter, and we can say with Joseph Fitzmyer that 'the inscription is the only thing to our knowledge to have been written about Jesus during his earthly life'.[85] Since it was public, it cannot have been an invention of the first Christians: since the title 'king of the

Jews' was attributed to monarchs like Alexander Jannaeus and
Herod the Great, it had no messianic or any other connotations in
the theology of the primitive church.[86] Perhaps fixed to the cross,
though there is no attestation of this usage, the placard was at
least carried in front of the condemned man or hung around his
neck, as is the case in the several examples provided by the
historians of antiquity.[87] We may regard Mark's brief formula as
being the best guarantee,[88] the others seeming to be later
elucidations. Doubtless scribbled hastily on a papyrus sheet,
these few words are nevertheless of the utmost importance to
anyone who wants to penetrate the reality of what happened.
Rudolf Schnackenburg[89] has given an excellent paraphrase of
them: 'This Jesus of Nazareth is guilty of death because as "king
of the Jews" he has rebelled against the Roman empire.'

Mockeries

The scene of taunts of which Jesus is the object on Calvary (Mark
15.29–32 par.) includes biblical reminiscences: moreover it is
closely built into the account of the passion and draws on the
previous context in Mark. The allusion to the temple takes up the
Jewish trial, and the ironic title 'king of Israel' refers back to the
'king of the Jews'[90] of the Roman trial. It is plausible that,
deliberately exposed to the public gaze, crucified men had to put
up with sarcastic comments from them. But are not some
members of the senior clergy,[91] as described by the Gospels, out
of place in indulging in this cruel game, which was more the sport
of common people? We can ask ourselves this question and
wonder whether their involvement here is not more the natural
and literary extension of their role in the trial. As for the insults
which Jesus' companions are said to have uttered against him
(Mark 15.32b par. Matt.27.44) – leaving aside the possibility
that they were distracting themselves from their own torment –
we can ask why they should have had such an attitude. It could
well simply have been required by the need to end up with the
schematic number three: after the passers-by and the high priests,
the other men on their crosses join in this scene of opprobrium.

'Last words'

The Christian tradition, relayed by art, knows seven sayings of Jesus on the cross. It is not at all surprising that the Gospels should have thought it useful for their readers to follow the custom of the 'last words'. Distributed over the four Gospels, all these words are both instructing and edifying. Only one of the sayings surprises the Christian reader: the first words of Ps.22 in fact do not at all seem to serve the purpose I have just indicated. In crying out 'My God, my God, why have you forsaken me?', Jesus, according to the first two Gospels, gives a different impression from what is suggested by the context, in which his relationship with God would seem to be quite different. We can understand why Luke preferred to omit this prayer, which his Greek readers could easily have seen as a cry of despair. Mark and Matthew have done nothing to tone down a possible surprise, since they saw this prayer as the climax of a 'dereliction' which began at Gethsemane but which, because this time God was its author, did not in any way affect the religious purity of Jesus: abandoned in the hands of his adversaries, at this supreme moment Jesus turns towards God and in so doing realizes the prophecies which the beginning of the psalm resembles.

But was this prayer really pronounced by Jesus on the cross? At all events, one thing is certain: it was not invented by the evangelist Mark. That does not follow from its 'scandalous' nature – had Mark seen it in this light he would not have reported it – but from the fact that this prayer is quoted in Aramaic. Mark is writing for readers who do not know that language, and when he quotes sayings of Jesus or other phrases in Aramaic,[92] he immediately translates them into Greek. In the present instance, as in other instances of the same kind, the natural explanation is that here we have the heritage of a tradition derived from Aramaic-speaking Jewish Christian circles in Palestine.

However, that does not guarantee the historicity of the prayer. One doubt arises from the fact that the Psalm in question is referred to twice more in the same context (Mark 15.24,29),[93]

and that it is one of the main scriptural references in the account
of the passion. The fact that it is quoted in Aramaic[94] before
being translated into Greek could lead the exegete here to
recognize a *cri du coeur*, certainly borrowed from scripture but
which, pronounced in the familiar dialect, goes beyond all
convention. However, even supposing that someone present had
recorded the prayer on the lips of Jesus in his agony and then
communicated it to his disciples, we must not forget that in Mark
this is not the only time when Aramaic words are attributed to
Jesus. The first Palestinian developments of scriptural apologetic
were well capable of resorting one last time to this 'messianic'
psalm to make it a prayer of Jesus on the cross, and of seeing his
lament in faith[95] as the realization of a programme which had
been fixed by God in the holy books.

This prayer ends in derision, and the Markan text combines
this derision with the act of a bystander, who gives Jesus a drink.
However, if a soldier's gesture of putting a soaked sponge to the
lips of the crucified Christ is quite plausible, as we shall see, we
cannot say the same thing of the play on words which ac-
companies it.[96] Aramaic-speaking listeners could not have
recognized the name of Elijah (*Eliyyah*) in an appeal to God
(*Elâ[h]i*). And the soldiers, who were capable of making such a
mistake, were pagans used to calling on the gods for help, but not
the prophet Elijah.[97] Hence the probability of the explanation
which sees this poor play on words as the work of the first
Christian Greek-speaking redactors,[98] working on the basis of a
vague similarity. In so doing they gave the act of offering Jesus
something to drink a cruel irony. By quenching Jesus' thirst, the
person offering the drink was prolonging his life, thus giving
'Elijah' time to intervene: a vain attempt, since Jesus died
immediately afterwards.

Jesus is given a drink

According to the four evangelists,[99] the 'vinegar' which Jesus is
given before he dies is an additional piece of cruelty and the
fulfilment of a scriptural prophecy (Ps.69 [LXX 68].22). In fact

such a gesture, while quenching the burning thirst of the crucified man, could delay his end,[100] and thus be a sign of the sadism rather than the compassion of the executioners. This 'vinegar' is seen as the acidulated drink called *posca*, a mixture of water, eggs and vinegar, used by soldiers and workers in the fields.[101] That Jesus had to be offered this in a sponge put at the end of a spear,[102] a spontaneous comment without the slightest theological impact, could well derive from an eye-witness.

The death of Jesus

We must leave it to medical science to identify the immediate physiological cause of the death of Jesus,[103] and to commentaries on the Gospels to give meaning to the second cry which, according to the Synoptics (Mark 15.37), Jesus will have uttered before expiring; at all events, such an effort is incompatible with the state of total exhaustion in which the crucified Jesus then was.

Exploited for its symbolism by John (19.31–37), the only evangelist to bear witness to it, the scene of the spear thrust is no less the echo of real facts, stemming in the last analysis from a visual experience.[104] Usually the Romans left the bodies of the crucified unburied and under guard.[105] A prisoner, having implored Octavius to allow him to be buried, was told that 'this would soon be a matter for the vultures'.[106] We also know the example of the martyrs of Lyons (in 177), whose torn bodies remained six days in the amphitheatre before they were burned and their ashes were thrown into the Rhone, despite the efforts of the families to persuade or bribe the guards.[107] The bodies of the Christians beheaded in Palestine on 13 November 309 had no right to burial: guarded day and night, they were devoured by the wild animals.[108] However, exceptions are noted: Philo[109] mentions the case of executed men who were brought down dead from their crosses at the approach of the festival of the emperor's birthday. That a delegation of Jews – one might envisage some of the nobility, indeed members of the Sanhedrin – went to the praetorium to ask Pilate to have the crucified men finished off at the approach of the sabbath (John 19.31) is an entirely neutral matter, which moreover conforms with Jewish feelings, according to the rule in Deuteronomy (21.23) which requires the body of a criminal to be taken down from the gibbet and buried before nightfall.[110]

Those who were crucified often suffered a long agony.[111] To bring on death the soldiers used the *crurifragium*,[112] breaking the legs of the crucified men with iron bars: this caused the body to slump and brought on death by asphyxia. Unlike his companions, Jesus already seems to the soldiers to be dead. To be more certain, one of them puts his spear in his side, certainly the left side, to reach the heart.[113]

'Blood and water' then flow from the wound. That is how the Gospel of John presents it in a passage which no doubt derives from a secondary redaction.[114] That neither weakens nor confirms the history of this detail, the observation of which, according to the same passage, is the act of an eye-witness. Rather than being a miracle, which would truly be amazing in this part of the Gospel,[115] the phenomenon, exploited for its symbolism, has good guarantees for its reality. We must leave it to medical experts to describe the approximations of the text in technical language,[116] drawing from them sufficient support for the choice which has just been made.

The women witnesses

The four evangelists mention the presence of women disciples in the context of the death of Jesus.[117] According to the Synoptic Gospels, they keep their distance as they watch what happens on Calvary.[118] This position is certainly more probable than their place at the foot of Jesus' cross which John offers us, with no regard for the executioners responsible for guarding the executed men. It is hard to see how they would have tolerated a group of women close to them. Moreover, by introducing the mother of Jesus and the 'disciple whom Jesus loved' into the group, John indicates that for him this is a scene of great importance; however, it remains highly problematical whether it took place here and in these circumstances.[119]

8

The Burial

As I recalled in the previous chapter, the Roman rule was that those who had been crucified, once dead, should remain on the cross. The Fourth Gospel (John 19.31) reports an approach to Pilate by prominent Jews with the request that Jesus and his fellow-sufferers should be taken down from their crosses before the beginning of the sabbath.[1] The Synoptics do not know this episode and, like John later (19.38), record another approach to the governor, that of Joseph of Arimathea. We are told that he went in search of Pilate to ask him for the body of Jesus. This request was granted, and Joseph took Jesus down from the cross and proceeded to bury him. This version of the facts takes no account of the previous one and forms a partial doublet with it.[2] In fact, Joseph's request to Pilate derives from a schematization which attributes the whole approach to the same person. Centred solely on Jesus, it is historically less sure than a request relating to all those who had been executed, without distinction, of which John preserves the trace. We can perfectly well see how, following the request of the Jews, the soldiers, having caused or (in the case of Jesus) confirmed the death of the crucified men, would have brought them down from the crosses to which they had been fixed (they were equipped to do this). The ultimate fate of the bodies was no longer their concern, and since the usual rule had been waived, required no further permission from the governor.

All the Gospels attribute the honour of having buried Jesus to Joseph of Arimathea. The history of his person and his role in the matter are undeniable: without doubt both figured among the memories of the first Jerusalem community. The man came from a place the Greek toponomy of which relates, as various indications demonstrate,[3] to the present village of Rantis (around eighteen miles north-east of Jerusalem, around the level of Jaffa), biblical Ramathaim, which makes Joseph a compatriot of Samuel (I Sam.1.1).

Joseph is presented in Matthew (27.57) as a disciple of Jesus. More specifically, John (19.38) makes him a crypto-disciple, like Nicodemus (3.2; 19.39).[4] That he was a disciple is completely passed over in silence in Mark and Luke. The former simply notes that Joseph 'was awaiting the kingdom of God' (Mark 15.43), and Luke regards him as 'a good and just man' (Luke 23.50). The same evangelist make him a 'councillor' (*bouleutês*), and if Mark leaves some doubt about the precise significance of the term,[5] Luke shows that he has understood it as 'member of the Sanhedrin' by adding that Joseph 'had not consented to their purpose and deed' (23.51), i.e. of the members of the Sanhedrin who had condemned Jesus. For Mark (15.43) the man is '*euschêmôn*', which could be rendered as 'eminent' or 'influential'. Matthew (27.57) makes him a 'rich man'.

This last detail accords with the fact that Joseph, again according to Matthew, had a brand new tomb which he had made for himself in the rock. Luke (23.53) and John (19.41) also emphasize the fact that this was the first time that the tomb was used. Neither Matthew (27.59) nor Luke (23.53) add anything to Mark about the funeral preparations. John, on the other hand, makes good this lack with an extraordinary profusion of spices[6] and the wrapping of Jesus' body in linen cloths. None of the canonical Gospels[7] mentions an inalienable custom, the washing of the dead body. Apart from John, these Gospels leave us with the impression of a rapid action, which omitted a large number of the most basic obligations that were a prelude to burial.

We can now draw some conclusions from the preceding remarks.

After the bodies of Jesus and his fellow-sufferers had been taken down from the crosses by the soldiers, Joseph was one of those who proceeded to bury them.[8] According to Deuteronomy (21.22–23), which prescribes that the body must be buried before sunset,[9] this was obligatory. Joseph is presented in Mark and in Luke as a pious Jew,[10] and we can grant that he was intent on accomplishing this act of faithfulness to the law. On the other hand, we cannot say whether he was also moved by some attachment to Jesus, since the earliest tradition is silent on the subject. At all events he was not a disciple of Jesus, but intervened in the absence of the kinsfolk who would normally have undertaken this office, and in the present case in the absence of Jesus's women companions, who still kept their distance from the executed men for a reason that we cannot identify more closely – fear on their part? Were they harassed by the soldiers or the Jews?

According to the Old Testament, those condemned to death could not be buried in the tomb of their ancestors.[11] Flavius Josephus evokes the case of Achan (Josh.8.29): having been stoned, at nightfall he had the right only to 'the dishonourable [*atimos*] burial reserved for those who have been condemned'.[12] But Josephus adds this last detail to the Bible, just as elsewhere he supplements the regulation in the Torah when he writes: 'Let him who has committed a blasphemy against God be stoned, then let him be hung up for a day and be buried without honour and obscurely [*atimôs kai aphanôs*].'[13] The practice customary in the author's day is presented here. It was to be codified in the Mishnah,[14] which specifies that those condemned to death may not be buried in the family tomb, but that the courts must make grounds[15] available for them. Only later, when their bodies have decomposed, can their bones be gathered and 'repatriated'.[16]

Mark's account, which is the tersest, suggests that Jesus did not enjoy any privileges here, either the washing of his body or anointing, whereas one would suppose that a worthy burial would have included these.[17] Whoever was responsible must have been content to wrap the corpse of Jesus in a shroud, a minimum requirement given the Jewish repulsion at the naked body.[18] It was then put in some 'tomb'. According to Mark, who is the most matter-of-fact on this question, the closing of the sepulchre – necessary to keep out animals – was basic: 'a stone' rolled in front of the entrance.[19] Given that Passover was like the holy day of rest, we might recall the prohibition in the Mishnah[20] against carrying a body on a bier and deduce from it that Jesus was buried close to the place of execution. At all events archaeology supports this localization, since as I have already pointed out,[21] excavations have brought to light several first-century Jewish tombs around the Holy Sepulchre. Without doubt one of them was the tomb in which Joseph of Arimathea placed the body of Jesus.

Abbreviations

AB	Anchor Bible
AGG	Aggelos
AGSU	Arbeiten zur Geschichte des Spätjudentums und Urchristentums
ApCA	Apocrypha, le champ des apocryphes
AThANT	Abhandlungen zur Theologie des Alten und Neuen Testaments
BA	*Biblical Archaeologist*
BaL	Bampton Lectures
BETL	Bibliotheca Ephemeridum Theologicarum Lovaniensium
BHist	Bibliothèque historique
Bib	*Biblica*
BiBe	*Biblische Beiträge*
BiKi	*Bibel und Kirche*
BPAA	Bibliotheca Pontificii Athenaei 'Antonianum'
BWANT	Beiträge zur Wissenschaft vom Alten und Neuen Testament
BZ	*Biblische Zeitschrift*
CaEL	*Cahiers Évangile et liberté*
CBQ	*Catholic Biblical Quarterly*
CCSL	Corpus Christianorum. Series latina
CPL	Cambridge Paperback Library
CQR	*Church Quarterly Review*
CRINT	Compendia Rerum Iudaicarum ad Novum Testamentum
CUFr	Collection des universités de France
DACL	*Dictionnaire d'archéologie chrétienne et de liturgie*
DBS	*Dictionnaire de la Bible. Supplément*
Dtb	Dalp Taschenbücher
EHPR	*Études d'historie et de philosophie religieuses*

OPLA	Les oeuvres de Philon d'Alexandrie
ÖTKNT	Ökumenischer Taschenbuch-Kommentar zum Neuen Testament
ParD	*Parole de Dieu*
PEQ	*Palestine Exploration Quarterly*
PG	Migne, *Patrologia Graeca*
PL	Migne, *Patrologia Latina*
QD	Quaestiones disputatae
QueSJ	Que sais-je?
RA	*Revue apologétique*
RAC	*Reallexikon für Antike und Christentum*
RAr	*Revue archéologique*
RB	*Revue biblique*
RBPhH	*Revue belge de philologie et d'histoire*
REJ	*Revue des études juives*
ReSR	*Recherches de science religieuse*
RHPhR	*Revue d'histoire et de philosophie religieuses*
RNT	Regensburger Neues Testament
RPh	*Revue de philologie*
RTL	*Revue théologique de Louvain*
SBA	Stuttgarter Biblische Aufsatzbände
SBFLA	*Studii biblici franciscani liber annuus*
SBT	Studies in Biblical Theology
SC	Sources chrétiennes
SNTS.MS	Society for New Testament Studies. Monograph Series
SNTU	Studien zum Neuen Testament und seiner Unwelt
SPAW.PH	*Sitzungsberichte der Preussischen Akademie der Wissenschaften. Philosophisch-historische Klasse*
SPIB	Scripta Pontificii Instituti Biblici
StANT	Studien zum Alten und Neuen Testament
StE	Studia evangelica
StJu	Studia Judaica
StPa	Studia Patavina
Stpb	Studia post-biblica
StTh	Studia theologica
StuBA	Stuttgarter Biblische Aufsatzbände
TCo	Theological Collections
TD	*Theology Digest*
TDNT	*Theological Dictionary of the New Testament*
TeSa	*La Terre sainte*

TG	*Theologie und Glaube*
ThA	Theologische Arbeiten
ThBei	Theologiche Beiträge
ThK	Theologischer Kommentar
TS	*Theological Studies*
TU	Texte und Untersuchungen
TZ	*Theologische Zeitschrift*
VC	*Vigiliae Christianae*
VD	*Verbum Domini*
WdF	Wege der Forschung
WUNT	Wissenschaftliche Untersuchungen zum Neuen Testament
ZDPV	*Zeitschrift des deutschen Palästina-Vereins*
ZNW	*Zeitschrift für die neutestamentliche Wissenschaft*
ZTK	*Zeitschrift für Theologie und Kirche*

Select Bibliography

Aischer, G., *Der Prozess Jesu*, KST 3, Bonn and Cologne 1929, reprinted Amsterdam 1963

Bammel, E., 'The Trial Before Pilate', in E.Bammel and C.F.D.Moule (eds.), *Jesus and the Politics of his Day*, 415–51
—— (ed.), *The Trial of Jesus. Cambridge Studies in Honour of C.F.D.Moule*, SBT II 13, London 1970
—— and Moule, C.F.D., *Jesus and the Politics of his Day*, Cambridge 1984
Barbet, P., *La Passion du Christ selon le chirurgien*, Paris [7]1965
Barrett, C.K., *The Gospel According to St John*, London 1965
Bauer, W., *A Greek-English Lexicon of the New Testament and Other Early Christian Literature*, English edition by W.F.Arndt and F.W.Gingrich, Cambridge and Chicago 1957, second revised edition Chicago 1979
Beilner, W., *Christus und die Pharisäer. Exegetische Untersuchung über Grund und Verlauf der Auseinandersetzungen*, Vienna 1959
Benoit, P., 'Jésus devant le sanhédrin', *Augustinianum* 20, 1943, 143–65; *Exégèse et théologie* I, Paris 1961, 290–311
——, 'Prétoire, Lithostroton et Gabbatha', *RB* 59, 1952, 531–56; *Exégèse et théologie* I, Paris 1961, 316–39
Betz, O., 'Probleme des Prozess Jesu', *Aufstieg und Niedergang der römischer Welt* II, 25.1, 565–647
Blinzler, J., *The Trial of Jesus. The Jewish and Roman Proceedings against Jesus Christ Described and Assessed from the Oldest Accounts*, Westminster, Maryland 1959
Brandon, S.G.F., *Jesus and the Zealots*, Manchester 1967
——, *The Trial of Jesus of Nazareth*, London 1968
Braun, F.-M., 'La sépulture de Jésus', *RB* 45, 1936, 34–52
Brecht, C.H., *Perduellio. Eine Studie zu ihrer begrifflichen Abgrenzung*

im römische Strafrecht bis zum Ausgang der Republik, MBPAR 29, Munich 1938

Broer, I., *Die Urgemeinde und das Grab Jesu. Eine Analyse der Grablegungsgeschichte im Neuen Testament*, StANT 31, Munich 1972

Brown, R.E., 'The Burial of Jesus (Mark 15.42–47)', *CBQ* 50, 1988, 233–45

——, *The Gospel according to John*, AB 29 (2 vols), Garden City, New York and London, 1966–1971

Büchler, A., 'L'enterrement des criminels d'après le Talmud et le Midrasch', *REJ* 46, 1903, 74–88

Bultmann, R., *The Gospel of St John*, Oxford 1971

——, *The History of the Synoptic Tradition*, Oxford ²1968

Burkill, T.A., 'The Trial of Jesus', *VC* 12, 1958, 1–18

Catchpole, D.R., 'The Problem of the Historicity of the Sanhedrin Trial', in E.Bammel (ed.), *The Trial of Jesus*, 47–65

——, *The Trial of Jesus: A Study in the Gospels and Jewish Historiography from 1770 to the Present Day*, Stpb 18, Leiden 1971

——, 'The "Triumphal" Entry', in E.Bammel and C.F.D.Moule (eds.), *Jesus and the Politics of his Day*, 319–34

Chardot, J.-L., *Jésus et sa mort dans l'évangile de Marc*, Faculté de théologie de Lyon 1968

Charlesworth, J.H., (ed.), *Jesus' Jewishness: Exploring the Place of Jesus within Early Judaism*, New York 1991

Cohn, H., *The Trial and Death of Jesus*, London 1972

Cothenet, E., 'L'attitude de l'Église naissante à l'égard du temple de Jérusalem', *Liturgie de l'Église particulière et liturgie de l'Église universelle, Conférence Saint Serge, XXIIᵉ Semaine d'études liturgiques, Paris, 30 juin–3 juillet 1975*, Rome 1976, 89–111

Cousin, H., *Le Prophet assassiné. Histoire des textes évangéliques de la Passion*, Paris 1976

Dabrowski, E., 'The Trial of Jesus in Recent Research', *StE* 4/1, TU 102, Berlin 1968, 21–7

Dalman, G., *Grammatik des jüdisch-palästinischen Aramäisch . . . Aramäische Dialektproben*, Leipzig 1927, reprinted Darmstadt 1960

——, *Sacred Sites and Ways. Studies in the Topography of the Gospels*, London 1935

——, *Jesus-Jeshua. Studies in the Gospels*, London 1929

Dautzenberg, G., 'Über die Eigenart des Konfliktes, der von jüdische Seite im Prozess Jesu ausgetragen wurde', in I.Broer (ed.), *Jesus und das jüdische Gesetz*, Stuttgart 1992, 147–72

Deissmann, A., *Light from the Ancient East*, London 1910

Denaux, A., 'L'hypocrisie des pharisiens et le dessein de Dieu. Analyse de Lc, XIII, 31-33', in F.Neirynck (ed.), *L'Évangile de Luc, problèmes littéraires et théologiques. Mémorial Lucien Cerfaux*, BETL 32, 1973, 245–85

Dodd, C.H., *The Founder of Christianity*, London 1971

——, *Historical Tradition in the Fourth Gospel*, Cambridge 1963

Dubois, J.-D., 'Les "Actes de Pilate" au IVe siècle', *La Fable apocryphe* II, ApCA 2, Turnhout and Paris 1991, 85–98

Dupont, J., 'Il n'en sera pas laissé pierre sur pierre (Mc 13,2; Lc 19, 44)', *Bib* 52, 1971, 301–21 = id., *Études sur les évangiles synoptiques* I, BETL 70A, 1985, 434–53

Ernst, E., *Das Evangelium nach Markus*, RNT, 1981

——, 'Die Passionserzählung des Markus und die Aporien der Forschung', *TG* 70, 1980, 160–80

Fitzmyer, J.A., 'Crucifixion in Ancient Palestine, Qumran Literature, and the New Testament', *CBQ* 40, 1978, 493–513

——, *The Gospel According to Luke*, AB 28–28a (2 vols), Garden City, New York 1983–85

Gaston, L., *No Stone on Another: Studies in the Significance of the Fall of Jerusalem in the Synoptic Gospels*, NT.S 23, 1970

Giblet, L., 'Un mouvement de résistance armée au temps de Jésus?', *RTL* 5, 1974, 409–26

Gnilka, J., *Das Evangelium nach Markus*, EKKNT 2/1–2 (2 vols), Zurich and Neukirchen 1978–79

——, *Jesus von Nazareth. Botschaft und Geschichte*, ThK III, Freiburg im Breisgau 1990

——, 'Der Prozess Jesu nach den Berichten des Markus und Matthäus mit einer Rekonstruktion des christlichen Verlaufs', in K.Kertelge (ed.), *Der Prozess gegen Jesu*, 11–40

Goguel, M., 'À propos du procès de Jésus', *ZNW* 31, 1932, 289–301

——, 'Le Procès de Jésus', *FV* 47, 1959, 395–403

——, *The Life of Jesus*, London 1933

Hengel, M., *Crucifixion in the Ancient World and the Folly of the Message of the Cross*, London and Philadelphia 1977

——, *Was Jesus a Revolutionist?*, Philadelphia 1971

——, *The Zealots. Investigations of the Jewish Freedom Movement in the Period from Herod I until AD 70*, Edinburgh 1989

Hoehner, H.W., *Herod Antipas*, SNTS.MS 17, Cambridge 1972, reprinted as *Herod Antipas: A Contemporary of Jesus Christ*, Grand Rapids 1980

Holzmeister, U., 'Crux domini atque crucifixio, quomodo ex archaeologia Romana illustrentur', *Verbum Domini* 14, 1934, 149–55; published separately, SPIB, Rome 1934 (which is cited here)

Imbert, J., *Le Procès de Jésus*, QueSJ 1896, reprinted Paris 1984

Jaubert, A., *Calendrier biblique et liturgie chrétienne*, EtB, Paris 1957

Jeremias, J., *The Eucharistic Words of Jesus*, London 1966

——, *Golgotha*, AGG 1, Leipzig 1926

——, *Jerusalem in the Time of Jesus*, London and Philadelphia 1969

——, 'Zur Geschichtlichkeit des Verhörs Jesu vor dem Hohen Rat', ZNW 43, 1950–51, 145-50

Jewish People in the First Century, The (ed. S.Safrai and M.Stern), CRINT, Section I (2 vols), Assen 1974–76

Juster, J., *Les Juifs dans l'Empire romain, leur condition juridique, économique et sociale* (2 vols.), Paris 1914, reprinted New York nd

Kertelge, K. (ed.), *Der Prozess gegen Jesus. Historische Rückfrage und theologische Deutung*, QD 112, Freiburg im Breisgau ²1989

Kopp, C., *Itinéraires évangéliques*, Paris 1964

Lampe, G.W.H., 'The Trial of Jesus in the "Acta Pilati"', in E.Bammel and C.F.D.Moule (eds.), *Jesus and the Politics of His Day*, 173–82

Légasse, S., 'Jésus devant le sanhédrin. Recherches sur les traditions évangéliques', *RTL* 5, 1974, 170–97

——, 'Jésus roi et la politique du IVe Évangile', in A.Marchadour (ed.), *Origine et postérité de l'évangile de Jean*, LeDiv 143, Paris 1990, 143–59

——, *Stephanos. Histoire et discours d'Étienne das les Actes des Apôtres*, LeDiv 147, Paris 1992

Lémonon, J.-P., *Pilate et le gouvernement de la Judée. Textes et monuments*, EtB, Paris 1981

Le Moyne, J., *Les Sadducéens*, EtB, Paris 1972

Léon-Dufour, X., 'Passion (Récits de la)', *DBS* VI, 1960, 1419–92

Lietzmann, H., 'Der Prozess Jesu', *SPAW.PH* 14, 1931, 313–22

Linnemann, E., *Studien zur Passionsgeschichte*, FRLANT 102, Göttingen 1970

Maier, J., 'Beobachtungen zum Konfliktpotential in neutestamentlichen Aussagen über den Tempel', in O.Broer (ed.), *Jesus und das jüdische Gesetz*, Stuttgart 1992, 173–213

Mara, M.G., *Évangile de Pierre, introduction, texte critique, tradition, commentaire et index*, SC 201, Paris 1973

Mommsen, T., *Das Römische Strafgericht*, Leipzig 1899

Müller, K., 'Möglickeit und Vollzug jüdischer Kapitalgerichtbarkeit im Prozess gegen Jesus von Nazareth', in K.Kertelge (ed.), *Der Prozess gegen Jesus*, 41–83

Neirynck, F., 'Anateilantos tou hêliou (Mc 16,2)', *ETL* 54, 1978, 70–103 = id., *Exegetica* I, BETL 60, Louvain 1982, 181–214

Nodet, E., 'Jésus et Jean Baptiste selon Josèphe', *RB* 92, 1985, 321–48

Parrot, A., *Golgotha and the Holy Sepulchre*, London 1957

Pelletier, A., 'L'Originalité du témoinage de Flavius Josèphe sur Jésus', *ReSR* 52, 1964, 127–203

——, 'Ce que Josèphe a dit de Jésus (Ant.XVIII 63–64)', *REJ* 4, 124, 1965, 9–21

Pesch, R., *Das Markusevangelium*, HThK 2/1–2 (2 vols), Freiburg im Breisgau 1976–80

Radl, W., 'Sonderüberlieferung bei Lukas? Traditionsgeschichtliche Fragen zu Lk 22, 67f; 23, 2 und 23,6–12', in K.Kertelge (ed.), *Der Prozess gegen Jesus*, 131–47

Rivikin, E., *What Crucified Jesus?*, Nashville and London 1984

——, 'What Crucified Jesus?', in J.H.Charlesworth (ed.), *Jesus' Jewishness*, 226–57

Robbins, V.K., 'The Reversed Contextualization of Psalm 22 in the Markan Crucifixion: A Socio-Rhetorical Analysis', in *The Four Gospels 1992. Festschrift Frans Neirynck*, BETL 100, II, 1992, 1161–83

Ruckstuhl E., *Die Chronologie des letzten Mahles und des Leidens Jesu*, BiBe NF 4, Einsiedeln 1963

——, 'Zur Chronologie des Leidensgeschichte Jesu', SNTU 10, 1985, 27–61; 11, 1986, 97–129 and id., *Jesus im Horizont der Evangelien*, StuBA 3, 1988, 177–9

—— 'Zur Frage einer Essenergemeinde in Jerusalem und zum Fundort von 7Q5', in B.Meyer (ed.), *Christen und christliches in Qumran?*, ES 32, Regensburg 1992, 131–7

Ruhland, M., *Die Markuspassion aus der Sicht der Verleugnung*, Eilsbrunn 1987

Sanders, E.P., *Jesus and Judaism*, London and Philadelphia 1985

Schein, B.E., 'The Second Wall of Jerusalem', *BA* 44, 1981, 21–6

Schenk, W., 'Der Passionsbericht nach Markus. Untersuchungen zur Überlieferungsgeschichte der Passionstradition', Gütersloh 1974

Schenke, L., *Studien zur Passionsgeschichte des Markus. Tradition und Redaktion in Markus 14*, 1–42, FB 4, Würzburg 1971

Schille, G., 'Das Leiden des Herrns: die evangelische Passionstradition und ihr Sitz im Leben', *ZTK* 52, 1955, 161–205

Schlosser, J., 'La Parole de Jésus sur la fin du Temple', *NTS* 36, 1990, 398–414

Schmithals, W., *Das Evangelium nach Markus*, ÖTKNT 2/1-2, Gütersloh and Würzburg ²1986

Schmittlein, R., *Circonstances et cause de la mort de Jésus*, Baden 1950

Schnackenburg, R., *The Gospel according to John* (3 vols), London 1968–82

Schneider, G., 'Gab es eine vorsynoptische Szene "Jesus vor dem Synedrium"?', *NT* 12, 1970, 22–9

——, 'The Political Charge against Jesus (Luke 23,2)', in E.Bammel and C.F.D.Moule (ed.), *Jesus and the Politics of His Day*, 403–14

Schürer, E., *The History of the Jewish People in the Age of Jesus Christ* (*175 BC– AD 135*), new edition revised and edited by G.Vermes and F.Miller, Edinburgh 1973–86

Schwarz, G., *Jesus und Judas. Aramäische Untersuchungen zur Jesus-Judas-Überlieferung der Evangelien und der Apostelgeschichte*, BWANT 123, Stuttgart 1988

Segal, A.F., 'Jesus the Jewish Revolutionary', in J.H.Charlesworth (ed.), *Jesus' Jewishness*, 199–225

Segalla, G., 'Gesù, profeta eschatologico della restaurazione di Israele', *StPa* 30, 1993, 83–102

Sherwin-White, A.N., *Roman Society and Roman Law in the New Testament, The Sarum Lectures 1960–1961*, Oxford ³1969

——, 'The Trial of Christ', in *Historicity and Chronology in the New Testament*, TCo 6, London 1965, 97–116

Soards, M.L., 'Oral Tradition before, in, and outside the Canonical Passion Narratives', in H.Wansbrough (ed.), *Jesus and the Oral Gospel Tradition*, Sheffield 1991, 334–50

Storme, A., 'Les Lieux saints évangéliques. Qu'en est-il aujourd' hui de leur authenticité? XII: Jerusalem', *TeSa*, March–April 1992, 59–75

[Strack,H.L. and]Billerbeck, P., *Kommentar zum Neuen Testament aus Talmud und Midrasch* (7 vols.), Munich 1956–61

Theissen, G., 'Die Tempelweissagung Jesu. Prophetie in Spannungsfeld von Stadt und Land', *Theologische Zeitschrift* 22, 1976, 144–50 = id., *Studien zur Soziologie des Urchristentums*, WUNT 19, Tübingen 1983, 142–59

Vanel, A., 'Prétoire', *DBS* VII, 1972, 513–54

Vincent, L.-H. and Abel, F.-M., *Jérusalem. Recherches de topographie, d'archéologie et d'histoire, II, Jérusalem nouvelle*, Paris 1914

Viviano, B.T., 'The High Priest Servant's Ear: Mark 14:47', *RB* 96, 1989, 71–80

Vogler, W., *Judas Iskariot. Untersuchungen zu Tradition und Redaktion von Texten des Neuen Testaments*, ThA 42, Berlin 1983

Wilson, W.R., *The Execution of Jesus*, New York 1970

Winter, P., *On the Trial of Jesus*, second ed. revised and edited by T.A.Burkill and G.Vermes, StJu 1, Berlin and New York 1974

Zumstein, J., 'Le Procès de Jésus', *Miettes évangéliques*, Monde B 25, Geneva 1991, 337–53 (first published in *CaEL* 71, 1989, 1–5)

Notes

Full bibliographical details of works cited in shorter form are given in the Bibliography

Introduction

1. P.Winter, *On the Trial of Jesus*, Berlin and New York 1974.
2. J.Blinzler, *The Trial of Jesus The Jewish and Roman Proceedings against Jesus Christ Described and Assessed from the Oldest Accounts*, Westminster, Maryland 1959. This is translated, with additions, from the second German edition, *The Trial of Jesus*, Regensburg 1955. A third German edition appeared in 1960.
3. See ibid., 185f.

1. *The Sources*

1. Justin, *Apology* 1, 35, 9; 48, 3 (on the acts sent to Tiberius by Pilate); Tertullian, *Apology* 21, 24: 'Pilate, already a Christian in his heart, gave an account to the emperor, who at that time was Tiberius, of everything concerning the Christ', see also 5.2; Eusebius, *HE* II, 2, 1–3. None of these writers had seen any kind of document from the chancellery, and Eusebius here seems to be dependent on Tertullian, see Dubois, 'Les "Actes de Pilate"', 91.
2. This document was part of the intense Christian apologetic of the time, which was particularly supported by the Acts of the martyrs. We can only guess at its content. However, according to an addition by Rufinus to his version of Eusebius's *Church History* (IX, 6), and Eusebius himself *HE* IX, 5,1), presenting the document as blaspheming Christ, it seems that its attacks were more on the divinity of Jesus than on his political and revolutionary activity. In that case, the Christian Acts of Pilate could have been composed against those produced by Maximin: cf. Lampe, 'Trial', 175–6. Cf. Eusbeius, *HE* I, 9,3–4; IX, 5,1.
3. Josephus, *Antt.* XVIII, 63–4, LCL, translated by L.H.Feldman, London and Cambridge, Mass.1965.
4. Ibid., XX, 200: on James, 'the brother of Jesus called Christ'. For

the intervention of a strange hand see H.St J.Thackeray, *Josephus, The Man and the Historian*, New York 1929, reprinted 1967, 143–4; Nodet, 'Jésus et Jean-Baptiste', 333–4.

5. I opt in part for the thesis recently put forward by C.Martin, 'Le *"Testimonium Flavianum"*. Vers une solution définitive?', *RBPhH* 20, 1941, 409–65. Pelletier ('L'Originalité', 'Ce que Josèphe a dit de Jésus') limits the glosses, first in the margin and then incorporated into the text, to two phrases put in italics in the translation above. For an acceptance of the whole of the *Testimonium Flavianum* as authentic see Nodet, 'Jésus et Jean-Baptiste', 331–41.

6. The argument has been refuted by Pelletier ('L'Originalité', 197–8; 'Ce que Josèphe a dit de Jésus', 12), who shows that this kind of ellipsis is usual in Josephus.

7. The word *endeixis* is vague. We find it twice more in Josephus, in *Antt.* XIII, 306 in the neutral sense of 'indication', and ibid. XIX, 133, in the sense of 'denunciation'. Nodet ('Jésus et Jean-Baptiste', 334) thinks that the ambiguity in the *Testimonium Flavianum* is intentional and that Josephus wanted to avoid *kategoria*, 'accusation' (see *Antt.* XVIII, 81, 139, 179, 250), which would reduce to some degree the part played by the high priests in the affair. But the nuance is minimal.

8. The title procurator is anachronistic for the time of Jesus. Down to Claudius, the title in Latin was *praefectus*, see 137 n.7. A benign interpretation of the expression *indicio eorum* is practically impossible, given the regular usage of *indicare, indicium*, in the sense of 'denounce', 'denunciation' (compare especially Tacitus, *Annals* II, 68; XV, 71, 2). J.Taylor (' "The Love of Many Will Grow Cold"; Matt.24: 9–13 and the Neronian Persecution', *RB* 86, 1989, 352–7) connects Matt.24.10–12 and Did.16.3–5 with the notice in Tacitus.

9. Nodet, 'Jésus et Jean-Baptiste'.

10. See a survey of these hypotheses in Blinzler, *The Trial of Jesus*, 33–4. For the possible use of the *Jewish Antiquities* by Tacitus, recently proposed by Nodet, see 'Jésus et Jean-Baptiste', 344–5. The thesis of any dependence of Tacitus on Josephus was refuted by E.Norden, 'Josephus und Tacitus über Jesus Christus und eine messianische Prophetie', *NJKA* 16, 1913, 637–66 = A.Schalit (ed.), *Zur Josephus-Forschung*, WdF 84, Darmstadt 1973, 27–69.

11. Suetonius, *Vespasian*, 6.6; Eusebius, *HE* III, 9,2.

12. Goguel, *The Life of Jesus*, 96.

13. W.Cureton, *Spicilegium Syriacum*, London 1855, 43–8. See the study of this document in Blinzler, *The Trial of Jesus*, 34–9.

14. Here again, as in Josephus, the king is described as 'wise', something which is understandable from a philosopher like Mara bar Serapion, who is trying to Hellenize teachers and doctrines for his readers (compare the description of John the Baptist in *Antt.* XVIII, 117).

15. See Josephus, *BJ* VII, 219–43.

16. bSanhedrin, 43a.

17. Baraita: a Tannaitic tradition not included in the Mishnah. This opinion derives from the fact that the phrase 'Jesus the Nazareth practised sorcery and led Israel astray' was introduced subsequently into another passage in the same treatise (b.Sanhedrin, 107b), giving a name, Yeshu, to the disciple of R.Joshua and creating remarkable confusion. Initially the disciple in question was anonymous, as is proved by the parallels in b.Sota 47a and j.Hagiga 2, 2 (77d 30). For possible reasons for the addition on Jesus in b.Sanhedrin 107b see [Strack-]Billerbeck I, 85; Blinzler, *The Trial of Jesus,* 24–5.

18. See Catchpole, *Trial,* 4–9.

19. The forty days of calling for a witness are meant to meet the accusation of a skimpy trial, or to put the crime of Jesus and consequently the justice of his condemnation beyond all question. The conventional figure 'forty' is also exaggerated and contradicts the procedure described in the Mishnah (Sanhedrin 3.8; 6.1), on which the proclamation of the herald in part nevertheless depends (ibid. 6,1 end).

20. But without depending on them, since none of the several allusions to Jesus in the Talmud allows us to suppose that its writers had access to the Gospel *texts,* and those who communicated to Jewish ears the attribution of Jesus' exorcisms to Beelzebul will not have been Christians.

21. There is the same use in Deut.13.6–7 and in the Talmud passage of the verbs *hiddîah,* 'turn aside' and *hesît,* 'seduce'. Justin (*Dialogue* 69,7) attests the same imputation by the Jews that in performing miracles Jesus was a 'magician' who 'led the people astray' *(magon . . . kai laoplanon).* See also Lactantius, *Divine Institutions* 5.3.

22. The title of this edition of the *Toledot Yeshu* is 'The Story of the Hung Man' (*Ma'aseh talûy*).

23. Blinzler, *The Trial of Jesus,* 26.

24. For the attribution of responsibility solely to the Jews see T.Reinach ('Josèphe sur Jésus', *REJ* 35, 1897, 1–18: 17): 'The Jews themselves, three or four centuries after the event, were imprudent enough to accept responsiblity for this alleged crime and even to boast of it.'

25. Voltaire, *Lettre sur les Juifs, Mélanges*, Collection La Pléiade, Paris 1965, 1212.

26. Against J.-P.Osier, *L'Évangile du ghetto ou Comment les Juifs se racontaient Jésus*, Paris 1984, 14. By contrast, contact by Christians and the influence of the preachers of the 'Jewish mission' explain some theological notes about the passion of Jesus: see G.Schlichting, *Ein jüdisches Leben Jesu. Die verschollene Toledot-Jeschu-Fassung Tam u- mu'ad*, WUNT 24, Tübingen 1982, 28–30.

27. S.Krauss, 'Une nouvelle recension hébraïque du Toldot Yêschû', *REJ* NS 3, 1938, 65–90: 67 for the first quotation; *Das Leben Jesu nach jüdische Quellen*, Berlin 1902 reprinted Hildesheim 1977, 237 for the second.

28. The word 'cross' appears only in Heb.12.2 and 'crucify' only in Acts 11.8.

29. The formula *epi Pontiou Pilatou* has a judicial scope, like those to be read in Mark 13.9; Matt.28.14; Acts 23.30; 24.20; I Cor.6.1 and elsewhere in non-scriptural Greek; cf. Bauer, *Lexicon*, 579–80.

30. For a list of objections to the authenticity of this passage see B.A.Pearson, 'I Thessalonians 2:13–16: A Deutero-Pauline Interpolation', *HTR* 64, 1971, 70–4; J.Coppens, 'Miscellanées bibliques. LXXX. Une diatribe antijuive dans I Thess. II, 13–16', *ETL* 51, 1975, 90–5. The absence of a comma between *tôn Ioudaiôn* and what follows in I Thess.2.14–15 (cf. F.D.Gilliard, 'The Problem of the Antisemitic Comma Between 1 Thessalonians 2.14 and 15', *NTS* 35, 1989, 481–502), while preventing the reader from attributing the murder of Jesus to the whole of the Jewish people, nevertheless does not rectify history, since the Romans are passed over in silence.

31. In this sense see above all M.Pesce, *Paolo e gli Arconti a Corinto. Storia della ricerca (1888–1975) ed esegesi di 1 Co 2, 6.8*, Brescia 1977 (esp.408–20), who gives a detailed presentation of the modern exegesis of this passage. Along the same line, but with less precision on the authorities put in question, see G.Miller, 'ARKHONTÔN TOU AIÔNOS TOUTOU – A New Look at 1 Corinthians 2: 6–8', *JBL* 91, 1972, 522–8; A.W.Carr, 'The Rulers of this Age – I Corinthians II.6–8', *NTS* 23, 1976–77, 20–35; G.D.Fee, *The First Epistle to the Corinthians*, NIC, Grand Rapids 1987, 103–4, 106–7.

32. Cf. Mara, *Évangile de Pierre*, esp. 30–3, 214; R.E.Brown, 'The Gospel of Peter and Canonical Gospel Priority', *NTS* 33, 1987, 321–43; J.B.Green, 'The Gospel of Peter: Source for a Pre-Canonical

Passion Narrative?', *ZNW* 78, 1987, 293–301. The quotation from Lampe which follows is from 'Trial', 176.

33. See 12f. above.

34. Cf. T.A.Burkill, 'St. Mark's Philosophy of the Passion', *NT* 2, 1958, 245–71: 247–8; id., *Mysterious Revelation: An Examination of the Philosophy of St Mark's Gospel*, Ithaca, NY 1963, 220–2.

35. Cf. also Gal.6.14; I Cor.1.23–24; Phil.2.8; Eph.2.16; Heb.12.2; I Peter 3.18 etc.

36. Léon-Dufour, 'Passion', 1429.

37. For a survey of opinions see, among others, E.Ernst, *Das Evangelium nach Lukas*, RNT, 1977, 643–4; Fitzmyer, *Luke* I, 1365–6; F.J.Matera, *Passion Narratives and Gospel Theologies: Interpreting the Scriptures through Their Passion Stories*, New York and Mahwah, NJ 1986, 152–5, 238–9.

38. See the examples illustrating this in Fitzmyer, *Luke* II, 1487–8, in connection with Luke 23.18–25 and in Radl, 'Sonderüberlieferung', 131–47.

39. Fitzmyer, *Luke* II, 1365.

40. For a good recent survey of the question see J.Beutler, 'Méthodes et problèmes de la recherche johannique aujourd'hui', in *La Communauté johannique et son Histoire*, Monde B, Geneva 1990, 15–38: 16–28.

41. For Matthew cf. John 18.11 and Matt.26.52a. In the two Gospels the name of the high priest, Caiaphas, is given (John 18.13–14, 24,28; Matt.26.3, 57); the name of Jesus appears on the inscription on Calvary (John 19.19; Matt.27.37); Joseph of Arimathea is described as a disciple (John 19.38; Matt.27.57); the tomb where he puts Jesus is 'new' *(kainos*, John 19.41; Matt.27.60). For Luke: Satan and Judas (John 13.2; Luke 22.3); the absence of a nocturnal trial; scourging to please the Jews (John 19.1; Luke 23.16, 22); the tomb of Jesus in which no one has yet been laid (John 19.41; Luke 23.63).

42. However, it must be pointed out that a good narrator is obliged to include some concrete details in his stories and to establish a certain logic: see above, 19f. (about Malchus and his kinsman) and 49 (about the disciple 'known to the high priest').

43. See Soards, 'Oral Tradition', 337–45. Among the most substantial elements one might think, in connection with Matthew, of the following facts: the negotations betwen Judas and the high priest (27.3–10); the intervention of Pilate's wife (27.19); Pilate's gesture of washing his hands in front of the crowd (27.24); the people's declaration of their responsibility (27.25); the opening of the tombs (27.52–53); the

guard on Jesus' tomb (27.62–66). In connection with Luke: Jesus' appearance before Herod Antipas (23.8–12); the words of the women weeping on the way to Calvary (23.27–31); the episode of the 'penitent thief' (23.39–43); Jesus' last prayer (23.46); the repentance of the crowd.

44. See the general survey of opinions in Ernst, 'Passionserzählung'. For the liturgical theories see C.Grappe, 'Essai sur l'arrière-plan pascal des récits de la dernier nuit de Jésus', *RHPR* 65, 1985, 105–25; 'D'un Temple à l'autre. Pierre et l'Église primitive de Jérusalem', *RHPR* 71, Paris 1992, 172–6.

45. It is hard to see how certain episodes could have circulated in isolation in the tradition. Thus the conversations between Judas and the high priests, the flight of the young man naked in Gethsemane, Peter's denials, the Barabbas affair and the intervention of Simon of Cyrene all are facts which call for a context, as Soards, 'Oral Tradition', 335–6, has emphasized.

46. For the scheme of preaching preserved in I Cor.15.3–4 see Ernst, 'Passionserzählung', 171–3. One thinks in particular of the two sources, one 'Roman' and the other 'Semitic', envisaged by V.Taylor (*The Gospel according to Mark*, London 1955, 653–64), a master of fragmentation on the basis of philological and stylistic arguments which when taken together all seem very arbitrary.

47. One can only approve of the way in which Cousin *(Le Prophète assassiné*, 145–9) already included miracles and reminiscences or scriptural quotations in the supposed 'primitive account of the crucifixion and death'.

48. See above, 80f.

2. The Arrest

1. For possible broader senses of the term to denote a plot of land where vegetables are grown see Dodd, *Tradition*, 67 n.4.

2. Cf. Dalman, *Grammatik*, 191; *Jerusalem und seine Gelände*, Gütersloh 1930, 179; *Sacred Sites and Ways*, 326–7.

3. Luke 6.12; 9.28.

4. For the meaning 'wait', 'stay' (and not 'meet') for the verb *synagesthai* here and in Acts 11.26 see H.Reynen, 'Synagesthai Joh 18,2', *BZ* NF 5, 1961, 86–90.

5. Here *ochlos* does not have the sense of 'crowd' of people but rather of 'band' or 'troop' as in Acts 1.15; 6.7 and elsewhere in Greek. For the

'clubs' *(xyloi,* 'wood', batons) as arms, see Josephus, *BJ* II, 176 (a police action by Roman soldiers on Pilate's orders); Eusebius, *HE* II, 23,18 (James killed by a blow from a stave, *xylon*).

6. For rabbinic legislation on this see Dalman, *Jesus-Jeshua*, 96–7; [Strack-] Billerbeck I, 995.

7. See 70–4 above.

8. For a bibliography see E.Lohse, 'Sabbaton', *TNDT* 7, 8–9.

9. 10.33; 11.18; 14.1 (high priests and scribes); 14.10; 15.3, 10, 11, 31 (high priests alone); 14.47, 53, 54, 60, 61, 63, 66 (the high priest).

10. In Acts 4.1, 'the priests, the governor of the temple and the Sadducees' come to arrest the apostles within the sanctuary.

11. Note that the Pharisees did not have 'servants' who could make an arrest, and the mention of them brings out the stereotyped designation of the Jewish opposition in John. On the question of the 'servants' in Josephus (*BJ* I, 655; *Antt.* XVI, 232): the word *hypêretês* denotes the executioner or torturer.

12. b.Pesahim, 57a; Tos.Menahot 13, 21.

13. Drafting decrees.

14. Translation from Jeremias (*Jerusalem,* 195–6), where a critical annotation of the famous complaint can be found.

15. Although Blinzler *(The Trial of Jesus,* 64–9) and Catchpole (*Trial,* 148–51) tried to prove the contrary. In the text there is a clear distinction between the Jewish guards and the *speira,* which moreover elsewhere in the New Testament (Mark 15.16 par. Matt.27.27; Acts 21.31) denotes the Roman cohort of Jerusalem (see also Acts 10.1; 27.1). The same goes for the 'chiliarch', Acts 21.31, 32, 33, 37. As well as the cohort, this 'part of the Roman garrison' comprised a contingent of cavalry, in all about 10,000 men.

16. Mark 14.10–11 par. Matt.26.14–16. For Matthew's version see above, 18.

17. For the origin of the surname 'Iscariot' see the account of theories in J.-A.Morin, 'Les Deux Derniers des Douze: Simone le Zélote et Judas Iskariôth', *RB* 80, 1973, 332–58: 349–58. The explanation developed by the author is based on distant Hebrew and Aramaic analogies which are by no means evident. Moreover, to account for the surname from the character and role of Judas comes up against the fact that his father – at least if one trusts the Fourth Gospel (John 6.71; 13.2, 26) already bore the same surname. It seems clearest that this is simply the transcription of *îsh Keriyyôt* ('man of Keriyyot'). In fact: 1. *îsh* is used in surnames: 2. places by the name of Keriyyot are known (Josh.15.25; Jer.48.24);

3. an ancient exegetical tradition, attested by several variants, replaced 'Iscariot' with the words *apo Karyôtou* ('from Keriyyot'). We can leave aside as totally improbable the thesis which makes Judas a figure entirely constructed by the first Christians as the embodiment either of Christian apostasy or (even worse) Judaism (because of the name 'Judas'!).

18. But does not Paul at the same time provide the main objection to Judas belonging to the group of Twelve? He writes that Jesus 'appeared . . . to the Twelve'. Should he not have written 'to the Eleven' (like certain correctors of the text)? But the traditional summary on the resurrection which Paul quotes here is using an official designation which was henceforth fixed in the language of the communities, whereas the 'Eleven' only appear among witnesses at the end of the second century or even later (Luke 24.9, 33; Acts 1.36; 2.14; Mark 16.14; Matt.28.16 has 'the eleven disicples'). Moreover, the group had been brought up to strength by the prompt election of Matthias (Acts 1.15–26, substantially historical).

19. See these lists in Mark 3.16–19 par. Matt.10.2–4; Luke 6.13–16. According to some authors, Judas' action against Jesus could even be the principal argument in favour of the formation of the group of Twelve by Jesus.

20. For Judas as the one who 'delivered up' Jesus, see Mark 3.19; 14.10, 11, 18, 21, 42, 44; Matt.10.4; 26.46, 48; 27.3, 4; Luke 22.4, 6, 21, 22, 48; John 6.64, 71; 12.4; 13.2, 11, 21; 18.2, 5; 21.20. For the judicial action at the end of which Jesus was to be put to death see Mark 9.31; 10.33; 14.41; 15.1, 10, 15, etc. In all these cases the expression is amplified by New Testament harmonies in which the plan of God is perceived (see Rom.4.25; 8.32). For the question see especially W.Popkes, *Christus traditus. Eine Untersuchung zum Begriff der Dahingabe im Neuen Testament*, ATANT 49, Zurich 1967. For the judicial action which was to be taken against the disciples see Mark 13.9, 11, 12; Matt.10.17, 19, 21; 24.9, 10; Luke 21.12, 16.

21. According to A.Schweitzer, *The Quest of the Historical Jesus*, London [3]1950, 394, the role of Judas will have consisted in transgressing the command to silence imposed by Jesus and telling the high priest of Jesus' claim to messianic royalty. This theory presupposes: 1. that the messianic secret in Mark is historical; 2. that Jesus defined his mission as messianic; 3. that this claim was the cause for the Jewish condemnation. Now none of these points is certain. In particular, as we shall see later, the account of the Sanhedrin session and the high priest's question about the messiahship of Jesus can in no way correspond to the

real facts. If it took place at all, Judas' conversation with the high priests will at most have consisted in spelling out how the arrest was to be made.

22. Among the less adventurous hypotheses one can cite the one which makes Judas disappointed in his hope of participating in a messianism of an active kind by following Jesus. Again, Jesus would have had to have kindled such a hope among those close to him in one way or another (see 65f. above.) On the term 'defection': I shall avoid speaking of 'betrayal' here since, as Ruhland (*Markuspassion*, 19) has reminded us, that 'could give the impression that Judas had passed on to the high priests a secret about Jesus, for example his plans or the place where he was staying'. Moreover only Luke (6.16) calls Judas a 'traitor' (*prodotês*), whereas neither the verb *paradidonai* which is used of Judas' action nor its Hebrew and Aramaic equivalents (*masar, mesar*) denote 'betrayal'. We may dismiss as fantastic the interpretation by Schwarz (*Jesus und Judas*, esp.228) according to which Judas gave up Jesus on the latter's orders. Unless we abuse the saying of Jesus in John 13.27b (see John 13.2), we are excused from attributing to him suicide by means of a third party.

23. The title 'rabbi' accompanying the gesture confirms its scope. For the significance of the kiss in the Bible and Judaism see A.Wünsch, *Der Kuss in Bibel, Talmud und Midrasch*, Breslau 1911; B.Meissner, 'Der Kuss im Alten Testament', *SPAW.PH* 1934, 914–30; M.Dibelius, 'Judas und Judaskuss', *Botschaft und Geschichte* I, Tübingen 1953, 272–7; [Strack-] Billerbeck, I, 995–6; G.Stählin, '*Phileô, ktl*', *TDNT* 9, 124–6, 136–44.

24. II Sam.20.9–10; Prov.27.6; Sirach 29.5.

25. Matthew (26.48) cancels this order; Luke passes over it in silence. For both of them, Jesus dominates the scene.

26. The diminutive *ôtarion* denotes the outer ear. The accident is quite plausible in the course of a scuffle, though Viviano ('The High Priest's Servant's Ear', 71–3) comments: 'To cut off the lobe of an ear and only the lobe, one has to hold the lobe with one hand and cut it off with a knife or a sword in the other.' Yes, if the operation is carried out by a surgeon.

27. According to M.-J. Lagrange (*Évangile selon saint Marc*, EtB, Paris [4]1947, 394), the narrator would be indicating that he knew the person. Brandon (*Trial* 77, cf. also 85 and 186 n.29) ses here a desire to clear the followers of Jesus and Jesus himself of the suspicion of rebellion. See also id., *Jesus and the Zealots*, 203, 206–9, 273, 322f.

28. Mark 14.69,70; 15.35,39.

29. For the shame and ridicule associated with having one's ear cut off see M.Rostovtzeff, '*Ous dexion apotemnein*', *ZNW* 33, 1934, 196–9; Viviano, 'The High Priest's Servant's Ear', 74–6. For the exclusion from the cult of those who had been mutilated see Lev.21.16–23; Josephus, *BJ* I, 259–70; *Antt.* XIV, 365–6 (Antigonus bites off the ears of Hyrcanus II to prevent him acceding to the high priesthood); Tos.Para 3.8 (Yohanan ben Zakkai cuts off the ear of a Sadducee for the same purpose). The term *doulos* which describes the victim of the sword blow in the four Gospel versions is intrinsically vague, and the writer could well intend it to be so, despite the article which governs it (the nuance in this case being: the servant of the high priest whose story the reader already knows; cf. Blinzler, *The Trial of Jesus*, 70 n.51 and compare 69 above). There is no need to envisage a special function, analogous to that of the 'king's servant' (II Kings 5.6). Far less need we see this man as the head of the troop, the '*strategos* of the temple' (Acts 4.1; 5.24,26), let alone the 'prefect of the priests' (*segan ha-kohanîm*) of whom the Mishnah speaks (though Viviano, 'The High Priest's Servant's Ear', 73, takes this line); the Mishnah designation does not correspond to that in the Gospels (for this figure see above, 25).

30. For the references in John see 1.41; 6.8, 68; 13.6, 9, 24, 36; 18. 10, 15, 25; 20.2,3; 21.2, 3, 7, 11, 15. Only Matt.16.16; Luke 5.8; II Peter 1.1 are to be added. The quotation comes from Dodd, *Tradition*, 79.

31. The name, with its variant 'Malikhos', occurs frequently in Josephus, in particular to denote the Nabateans. See the references in K.H.Rengstorf (ed.), *A Complete Concordance to Flavius Josephus. Supplement I, Namenwörterbuch zu Flavius Josephus*, by A.Schalit, Leiden 1968, 81. For the Semitic form of the name see T.Zahn, *Das Evangelium des Johannes*, KNT 4, Leipzig ³˒⁴1912, 619 n.12. This reference is very Johannine (John 4.46; 6.23; 12.9,17–18; 18.14; 21.20).

32. See above, 49.

33. An account and critique of 'the most adventurous speculations' can be found in F.Neirynck, 'La Fuite du jeune homme nu en Mc 14, 51–52', *ETL* 55, 1979, 42–66 = id., *Evangelica* I, BETL 50, Louvain 1982, 215–38. See also L.Sabourin (*L'Evangile selon saint Matthieu et ses principaux parallèles*, Rome 1978, 356), who thinks that 'the episode of the young man who flees naked ... can be explained quite naturally if he was the guardian of the place; he was sleeping in a hut and

the noise woke him'. Without denying Sabourin the right to imagine this, such a hypothesis does not take account of the fact that the person 'followed' Jesus. But is this detail, which makes the young man a kind of disciple, one of the original facts? Given the person's attire, one can doubt it. Note, moreover, the close parallel betwen the two phrases in Mark 14.50 and 14.52.

3. Why was Jesus Arrested?

1. Schürer, *History* II, 233–6.

2. Jeremias, *Jerusalem*, 175–81.

3. *BJ* VI, 114.

4. Ketubot 13.1–2; Ohalot 17.5.

5. See Jeremias, *Jerusalem*, 181 and 16 above.

6. A Sanhedrin made up solely of doctors of the Law and presided over by one of them is an invention of the rabbis, see Schürer, *History* II, 215–18.

7. According to Josephus (*Antt.* XVIII, 17), the Sadducees who became magistrates were forced to adopt Pharisaic views so as not to displease the people. For this passage, however, see the reservations of Le Moyne, *Les Sadducéens*, 43 and here, 68.

8. *BJ* II, 331, where we find the expression *tous te archiereis kai tên boulên* (which evokes Mark 14.55 par Matt.26.59).

9. In Greek he is designated *ho stratêgos tou hierou*, Josephus, *BJ* VI, 294; *Antt.* XX, 131; Acts 4.1; 5.24,26. The rabbinic documents call him *segan ha-kohanîm*: see Jeremias, *Jerusalem*, 160–3. The mere fact that *sagan* is translated *stratêgos* already says a good deal about the functions of the person concerned, which extended far beyond the strictly ritual sphere.

10. For the model reproduced in this episode see Catchpole, 'The "Triumphal" Entry'. By way of an example see the reconstruction of facts proposed by Gnilka (*Jesus von Nazareth*, 276; compare id., *Markus* II, 1119–20): Jesus arrives in Jerusalem as a pilgrim. Before the city gate he is hailed by his disciples and other pilgrims in terms which could have taken up the words of Ps.118. The joy aroused by arrival in the Holy City after a long journey is focussed on Jesus. One can also add to the acclamation the theme of the imminent coming of the kingdom of God, without excluding 'latent messianic tones'. The Romans did not react immediately, because 'the demonstration was peaceful'. E.P.Sanders (*Jesus and Judaism*, 306–9) reduces the demonstration to a

symbolic gesture in the manner of the prophets: performed before several disciples, it signified that Jesus claimed a royal dignity (as 'viceroy') in the imminent kingdom of God. But see above, 65f.

11. From a literary point of view Jesus' arrival at the temple is an extension of the triumphal entry: see Catchpole, 'The "Triumphal" Entry', 319–21.

12. Mark 11.15–17; Matt.21.12–13; Luke 19.45–56; John 2.14–22.

13. John 2.13,23; 5.1; 7.10.

14. This has been brought out well by Schnackenburg, *Gospel according to John* I, 343f.

15. On the basis of rabbinic documents it can be allowed that there were other shops on the slopes of the Mount of Olives. For this whole question see Jeremias, *Jerusalem*, 48–9.

16. This is the scene in John 2.15: 'And making a whip of cords, he drove them all, with the sheep and oxen, out of the temple'. See Dodd, *The Founder of Christianity*, 144–5.

17. This is part of the arsenal used to establish that Jesus was really an anti-Roman rebel. The radical thesis of R.Eisler (*IESOUS BASILEUS OU BASILEUSAS* II, Heidelberg 1930, 476–99) has been plagiarized by J.Carmichael, *The Death of Jesus*, London 1963, and other publications which are more concerned to be sensational than to be objective history. The more moderate thesis of S.G.F.Brandon (*Jesus and the Zealots*, especially 331–40) suffers from equally serious faults of method and historical inconsistencies (see Hengel, *Was Jesus a Revolutionist?*, 13–50). Particularly in the case of the incident at the temple, the nationalist interpretation of the event neglects the fact that on any hypothesis this was a Jewish sanctuary and not a Roman edifice, even taking account of the daily sacrifice offered for the prosperity of the emperor and his people.

18. See Hengel, *Was Jesus a Revolutionist?*, 27. For the special surveillance at feast times see Josephus, *BJ* II, 224–5; *Antt.* XX, 106–7.

19. See Bultmann, *History*, 36 and 389; also A.J.Harvey, *Jesus and the Constraints of History*, BaL, London and Philadelphia 1982, 132 and notes. Harvey objects that the phrase 'house of prayer for all nations' does not fit in with the Hebrew of the text that Jesus would have cited, and that moreover 'den of thieves' (*lêistai*) is not right here; one would have expected a term more like 'swindler'. This does not prevent Harvey from supporting the interpretation that Jesus was opposed not to the temple but to the current temple cultic practices.

20. Hengel (*Was Jesus a Revolutionist?*, 29 n.54) suggests as a hypothesis that this commentary should be attributed to 'the polemic of the Hellenists of Jerusalem against the temple, which had been linked with the words and example of Jesus (see Acts 6.13)'. I doubt the historicity of this charge in the 'trial' of Stephen (see my *Stephanos*, 20–2), since on this point Luke is dependent on Mark 14.58.

21. The second interpretation can be found in Dodd, *The Founder of Christianity*, 146–7; W.D.Davies, *The Gospel and the Land. Early Christianity and Jewish Territorial Doctrine*, Berkeley and Los Angeles 1974, 350–1 and n.46. See the quotation in Dodd, 147.

22. Unless one imagines Jesus making a scene in the narrow space of the court of the Israelites, or, on pretext of offering a sacrifice, in that of the priests.

23. Mark 2.27; 3.4; 7.1–23; 10.1–12; 12.18–27, 28–34 par.; Matt.5.20, 48; 23.16–26 par.

24. See M.Sheqalim 5, 45, on wine for libations. See also Jeremias, *Jerusalem*, 25–6.

25. Menahot 13,22.

26. For the order relating to cult objects see Schenck, *Passionsbericht*, 156, who refers to the Septuagint, where a quarter of the occurrences of the word *skeuos* denote cult objects. The main defender of the third interpretation is Sanders, *Jesus and Judaism*, 61–76. But see also Theissen ('Tempelweissagung', 144), for whom the incident in the temple and Jesus' words about its destruction express one attack on the temple in two different forms, envisaging its eschatological replacement.

27. For the details and the documentation see T.Reinach, *Les Monnaies juives*, Paris 1887; M.Lambert, 'Les Changeurs et la monnaie en Palestine', *REJ* 51, 1906, 217–44; 52, 1907, 24–42; I.Abrahams, *Studies in Pharisaism and the Gospels*, first series, Cambridge 1917 reprinted New York 1967, 82–9; A.Ben-David, *Jerusalem und Tyros. Ein Beitrag zur palästinischen Münz und Wirtschaftsgeschichte*, with a postscript, 'Jesus und die Wechsler', by Edgar Salin, Basel and Tübingen 1969; S.Safrai, *The Jewish People in the First Century* II, 879–81: E.Schürer, *History*, II, 66 and n.210, and 270–2.

28. This is the tax at issue in the episode of the 'didrachm' related in the Gospel of Matthew (17.24–27). It can hardly be used to argue that Jesus was disloyal to the current temple and its cult. Rather than being a recollection of the life of Jesus, it is in fact an echo of ancient discussions among Jewish Christians about the obligation to pay temple tax which Jesus, endowed with sovereign authority as master of the temple as of

the sabbath (Matt.12.6,8), is called on to settle. This is a theoretical freedom, which is in practice a concession to avoid useless conflicts with the Jews. Writing after 70, the evangelist derives a more general teaching from this composition.

29. The tax of a half-shekel provided for the regular sacrifices at the temple, Neh.10.33–34; M.Sheqalim 4, 1–3. So Jesus did not attack the market simply because that was all that there was in the Court of the Gentiles (which Sanders, *Jesus and Judaism*, 68–9, seems to be insinuating); the fact that he attacked the market as such has a special symbolism.

30. In the parable of the Good Samaritan (Luke 10.31–32), the priest and the Levite are only implicitly censured for their lack of pity towards the wounded man lying by the road.

31. In the Greek Bible, the verb *katastrephein*, above all as the equivalent of *hapak* (literally 'return'), often denotes the destruction of cities (like Sodom and Gomorrah in particular): Gen.13.10; 19.21, 25, 29; Deut.29.23 (22); Tobit 14.4; Sirach 48.14; Amos 4.11; 9.11; Jonah 3.4; Jer.20.16; 27 (Hebrew 50).40; 29 (Hebrew 49).18; Lam.4.6. See also Judg.7.13; II Chron.34.4; Job 12.14 (where it is opposed to *oikodomein*); Mal.1.14 (opposed to *anoikodomein*). Given these examples, the objection made by Sanders (*Jesus and Judaism,* 70) on the basis of the broken flask in Jer.19.10–12 loses its weight.

32. Thus J.Becker, 'Das Ethos Jesu und die Geltung des Gesetzes', in H.Merklein (ed.), *Neues Testament und Ethik, Festschrift R.Schnack-enburg*, Freiburg im Breisgau 1989, 31–52: 46.

33. To simplify these considerations and keep to essentials I shall leave the announcement of the 'abandoned house' (Luke 13.35 par Matt.23.38) out of consideration, since on the one hand the term 'house' (*oikos*), at least at the pre-Gospel stage, does not necessarily denote the temple but also the people or the city (see Jer.22.4–6; I Enoch 89, 50–56; Testament of Levi 10.5; 4Q Flor 1, 10, citing II Sam.7.11–44; thus Michel, '*Oikos ktl*', *TDNT* 5, 127 and n.27); on the other hand, the allusion to a *destruction* is not explicit.

34. The variants of Mark 13.2 in Matt.24.2; Luke 21.6 do not affect the sense of the oracle. Without prejudicing some personal interventions of the evangelist: the phrase in the genitive absolute, *kai ekporeuomenou autou* (Mark 13.1) is read as such in Mark 10.17, and *didaskale* on the lips of the disciples is a characteristic of the Second Gospel.

35. See I Kings 9.7–8; Jer.7.14; 26.6, 9, 18. See also I Enoch 90.28;

Josephus, *BJ* VI, 300–9; Testament of Levi 15.1; Targum Neofiti Lev 25,16 ('I shall destroy my sanctuary which is the force of your army' [or 'which is your powerful force']: in the form of a threat); j.Yoma VI, 43c, 61 par. b.Yoma 39b. For the whole issue see R.J.McKelvey, *The New Temple: The Church in the New Testament*, Oxford and New York 1969; Gaston, *No Stone*, esp.102–61; Sanders, *Jesus and Judaism*, 77–90.

36. The parallels are more remote in Micah 3.12; Jer.9.10, which predict the transformation of Jerusalem into 'a heap of stones', and in II Sam.17.13: 'We shall drag [this city] into the valley, until not even a pebble is left [*kataleiphthê*] there.'

37. See Dupont, 'Il n'en sera pas laissé pierre sur pierre', 310–19 or 443–52; Schlosser, 'La Parole de Jésus', 407–8.

38. See Gaston, *No Stone*, 15, 244, 356. See also Schlosser, 'La Parole de Jésus', 408.

39. Schlosser, 'La Parole de Jésus', 413–14.

40. The language of the quotation does not in itself exclude prophecy *ex eventu,* but its vagueness makes this less probable. To be persuaded of this we can compare this prophecy to that which Lactantius (*Divine Institutions* 4.21, cited by Gaston, *No Stone*, 45) attributes to Jesus and which has other details. At all events, Mark 13.2 is not enough to fix the composition of the Gospel after 70. On the other hand, it cannot be used to date it before the destruction of the city, let alone to confirm the attribution of the prophecy to Jesus, making use of the differences between this announcement and the reality of the facts. For while it is true that Josephus tells us that the temple was burnt (*BJ* VI, 249–87), he also writes (*BJ* VII, 1) that afterwards, 'Caesar, without further delay, ordered that it should be razed to the ground and tore down the whole city and the temple, leaving standing only the highest of the towers, Phasael, Hippicus and Mariamme, and the part of the rampart surrounding the city to the west.'

41. See Schlosser, 'La Parole de Jésus', 400–2.

42. See 94 above.

43. See S.Arai, 'Zum Tempelwort Jesu in Apostelgeschichte 6.24', *NTS* 34, 1988, 397–410: 398–9; Schlosser, 'La Parole de Jésus', 402–3; Légasse, *Stephanos*, 201–2. Against Sanders, *Jesus and Judaism*, 74, who envisages independent information obtained by the author of Acts from his sources.

44. The phrase is omitted in the recasting of the episode by Luke (see Légasse, 'Jésus devant le sanhédrin', 186–9). Matthew (26.61)

introduces important modifications here. Instead of 'I will destroy', he writes 'I can destroy', which both emphasizes the sovereign power of Christ over the temple and avoids attributing to him a destruction which is known to have been the work of the Romans. Moreover, 'this temple' is replaced by 'the temple of God', and the adjective *cheiropoiêtos* (made by human hands) and its opposite are suppressed: at the moment when Jerusalem is enduring the tragic consequences of the Roman conquest, Matthew continues to feel great respect for the 'holy city' (4.5; 27.53; cf. 5.35) and the sanctuary of which it is the extension.

45. For the kingdom as a metaphorical reconstruction of the temple see Gaston, *No Stone*, 161–2, 223–8. For the negative part, see J.R.Donahue, 'Temple, Trial, and Royal Christology (Mark 14.53–65)', in W.Kelber (ed.), *The Passion in Mark. Studies on Mark* 14–16, Philadelphia 1976, 61–79: 66–71.

46. Acts 7.48; 17.24; Enoch 9.11, 24 (see also II Cor.5.1). It is by no means unimportant that in the Septuagint the first of these terms serves to denote either the idols (Lev.26.1; Isa.46.6; also Sibylline Oracles 3, 606, 618) or the pagan sanctuary (Isa.16.1). Cf. E.Lohse, '*Cheiropoiêtos, acheiropoiêtos*', *TDNT* 9, 436. On the other hand there is no good reason for removing the 'three days' from this saying as a Christian addition, since the formula used on this occasion is not that used in connection with the resurrection: cf. J.Dupont, 'Ressuscité "le troisième jour" (I Co 15, 4; Ac 10, 40)', *Bib* 40, 1959, 742–61: 744 = *Études sur les Actes des apôtres*, Le Div 45, Paris 1967, 321–36: 323.

47. Taking account of the hesitations over the date of the Gospel of Mark.

48. For the addition of Mark 14.59 to the narrative see above, 40f.

49. See Cothenet, 'L'Attitude', 93–4, and the references. Sanders (*Jesus and Judaism*, 289) rightly reacts against the simplification which reduces the hostility towards Jesus to the leaders, but also against a restriction of popular sympathy for him solely to the Galileans. One is surprised to note that an author like Rivkin (*What Crucified Jesus?*, passim), who is sensitive to the political impact of the position of Jesus, totally fails to recognize what he says about the temple. If this is a point where the religious touches on the political, it is certainly a point where there is a challenge to the temple cult with its popular implications.

50. Jeremias, *Jerusalem*, 84, reckons that there were around 125,000 pilgrims for the Passover, though he notes that 'the number I arrived at could be halved'.

51. For the similar case of Jesus son of Ananias, who was also

brought before the governor of his time by the Jewish authorities for his prophecies of misfortune to the temple, see above, 54.

52. 'Methodologische Überlegungen zur Rückfrage nach Jesus', in K.Kertelge (ed), *Rückfrage nach Jesus. Zur Methodik und Bedeutung der Frage nach dem historische Jesus*, QD 63, Freiburg in Breisgau 1974, 11–77:42.

53. For the definitions of blasphemy to be found in the rabbis see [Strack-] Billerbeck I, 1002–19; H.W.Beyer, '*Blasphêmeo, ktl*', *TDNT* I, 621–2. The quotation is dervied from Sifre Num.112, on Num.15.30.

54. The criticism of the Torah which arises from the 'antitheses' in Matt.5.20–48 can as such only be the echo of the teaching of Jesus, and the parallel in Luke (6.47–38), where this criticism is lacking, confirms the Christian, indeed redactional, origin of this criticism.

55. For the problems of questions of food and the sabbath see Rom.14; Gal.4.10; Col.2.16,21. The argument of 'dissimilarity' from primitive Christianity which is used in favour of the authenticity of this saying of Jesus is thus hardly viable in this connection: see H.Räisänen, 'Jesus and the Food Laws: Reflections on Mark 7.15', in *Jesus, Paul and the Torah. Collected Essays*, JSNT.S. 43, Sheffield 1992, 127–48: 136. See Sanders, *Jesus and Judaism*, 264.

56. A remark made by Dautzenberg, 'Eigenart', 165.

57. John 19.7 is not an exception here, since the charge laid against Jesus does not relate to his attitude to the Law but to the fact that he thinks himself to be the Son of God. Those who anticipate by attaching too much importance to the murderous plan of the Pharisees and the Herodians against Jesus because he broke the sabbath (Mark 3.6) are making too much of a note which does not go back further than the composition of the Second Gospel. Moreover this would have been the case with Paul had he been judged and executed by the Jews, and was without doubt the case with Stephen. The charge cannot be extended to Jesus without going beyond the possibilities offered by the texts.

58. In Matt.27.62 the Pharisees intervene in the apologetic episode of the guard at the tomb which is peculiar to the First Gospel. For the addition of the Pharisees in 18.3 see above, 16.

59. Mark 14.1, 43, 53; 15.1; Luke 22.2, 66; 23.10; Matt.26.57; 27.41.

60. This defence, reported in two different forms in Mark 8.15 (par Matt.16.6) and Luke 12.1, is the only reasonably certain example of a criticism of the movement by the historical Jesus. The addition of the 'Herodians' in Mark (corrected to 'Sadducees' in Matthew) is not there

to clarify the scope of the attack. Matthew applies the 'leaven' to the doctrine of the Pharisees and Luke to their hypocrisy. What was its origin? The thesis that Jesus will have envisaged the influence of a purely political conception of the messianic kingdom (defended in particular by Hoehner, *Herod Antipas*, 202–8) has no more merit than others as a solution to this *crux interpretum*.

61. Matt.21.15–16; Luke 10.25; 15.2. See A.F.J.Klein, 'Scribes, Pharisees, High Priests and Elders in the New Testament', *NT* 3, 1959, 259–67; S.Légasse, 'Scribes – III Nouveau Testament', *DBS* XII, 277–9; id., '"Scribes et pharisiens". De l'anamnèse à Jésus', in *La Mémoire et le Temps. Mélanges offerts à Pierre Bonnard*, MondeB, Geneva 1991, 47–53.

62. Josephus, *BJ* XX, 200.

63. For the involvement of the Sanhedrin see above, 45–7. The weight of the Pharisees in the council, which was dominated by the priests, must not be overstated. See the remarks by Beilner, *Christus und die Pharisäer*, 236–7; Sanders, *Jesus and Judaism*, 312–18. The approach of the Pharisees reported in Luke 13.31 can be claimed as an indication of their benevolence towards Jesus only with considerably reservations. First of all, it is doubtful whether this approach was really inspired by a desire to save Jesus. At least, this is the view of the evangelists, who see the Pharisees only as 'hypocrites' (Luke 12.1), while Herod in Luke 23.8–11 shows no hostility towards Jesus. Here the Pharisees 'apparently . . . warn Jesus against the murderous intentions of Herod. In reality, they want to prevent Jesus from accomplishing his mission' (Denaux, 'Hypocrisie', 263). As for history, it takes a good deal of good will to see Luke 13.31 as anything other than a setting in which classical adversaries are used once again, though their role does not fit at all well with the final redaction.

4. *Jesus before the Jewish Authorities*

1. Here I am taking up in an abbreviated form, and with important modifications, my article 'Jésus devant le sanhédrin'.

2. The scene with the insults (Mark 14.65 par) is examined above, 47–9.

3. Mark 3.22–30; 5.25–34; 6.14–29; 11.15–19; 14.3–9.

4. Schneider, 'Szene', 34.

5. Isa.53.7; Ps.38.14–15.

6. Several authors dissect it more, regarding vv.57–59 as an insertion

(thus Bultmann, *History*, 270), which makes the high priest's question even more pointless than it is in the current text of Mark.

7. The verb *epseudomartyroun* thus leads from v.56 to v.57.

8. Some see verse 62 ('and you will see . . .') as an element added to smooth the transition from messianic ground to that of the apocalypses. This is an academic distinction, since in the Palestinian milieu in which this narrative appeared, it has hardly any *raison d'être*.

9. Deut.7.13–14; Ps.110 (LXX 109). 1.

10. The Fourth Evangelist (John 10.33), who depends, if not on this very passage, at least on the same tradition, understands it well when he makes the Jews declare: 'We stone you for no good work but for blasphemy; because you, being a man, make yourself God.'

11. Goguel ('À propos du procès de Jésus', 298; *Life of Jesus*, 509) thought that in not mentioning the resurrection, Jesus' reply attested its historicity. But how would it have been possible to speak of resurrection in a phrase addressed to the Jewish authorities and which begins with 'You shall see . . .?' In the Gospels, Jesus announces his resurrection only to the disciples, and the Easter appearances will be only to them.

12. The contact between Luke 22.67 and John 10.24–25 is a proof of Luke's independence from Mark only if John did not use the Synoptic Gospels, Luke in this instance. Moreover, the non-Lukan features of this verse (Semitic parallelism, *ean* and *ou me*) are reminiscences – in themselves very Lukan – of the Septuagint in Jer.45 (Hebrew 38).15.

13. After all, the association of Annas and Caiaphas is very clumsy, and indicates that the author does not have precise knowledge of the situation: in Luke 3.2, strictly speaking, the title of high priest, in the singular, denotes only Annas; in Acts 4.6, Caiaphas is relegated to a place among the members of the priestly families. See Dodd, *Tradition*, 93–4.

14. According to the context (18.13), the 'high priest' in 18.15, 19, 22 would have to be Caiaphas. Now it can only be Annas, since he is the one who sends Jesus to Caiaphas, who is also given the title of high priest (18.24). This is not to take into account the idea which the evangelist seems to have of the duration of the high priesthood (John 11.29; 18.13), which seems to be conceived of as 'an annual tenure, like that of priesthoods in the Greek cities' (Dodd, *Tradition*, 94 n.3, who nevertheless provides the evangelist with some excuses).

15. Dodd (*Tradition*, 95) is forced to confirm the historical probability of this interrogation on the basis of a *baraita* in the Talmud (b. Sanhedrin, 43a [his reference needs to be corrected]), according to which

Jesus was condemned to death for having 'practised sorcery, seduced Israel and led it astray'. For this text, which cannot be regarded as a historical tradition about Jesus, see 4f. above.

16. For teaching in the synagogues see Mark 1.21; 6.2; in the temple: Mark 12.35.

17. For the detail see Schnackenburg, *Gospel according to John* 3, 238. Catchpole's demonstration to the contrary (*Trial*, 8–9) cannot claim to establish that the dialogue between Annas and Jesus predates the Gospels.

18. For the saying on the temple (John 2.19) see above, 33; for the accusation of blasphemy (John 10.33), see 41. The contact between John 10.24–25 and Luke 22.67 was indicated on above, 11.

19. Some exegetes, following Syriac versions, have tried to resolve matters by inserting John 18.24 between 18.13 and 18.14, which makes it possible to attribute the question to Caiaphas. However, this comes up against the overwhelming testimony of the manuscript tradition.

20. In the New Testament see Luke 3.2; Acts 4.6; John 18.13, 24. In Josephus see *BJ* V, 506; *Antt.* XVIII, 26, 34; XX, 197–8. – The five sons of Annas were Eleazar (c.16–17), Jonathan (37), Theophilus (37–?), Matthias (under Agrippa I, 41–44), Hanan (Ananus) II (62), high priest for three months, who had James 'brother of the Lord' stoned. Matthias, son of Theophilus, was one of the last high priests (65–?). On the other hand it is not certain that the Jesus nominated by Archelaus a little before his dismissal was the brother of Annas, since the names of the fathers according to the Greek equivalent given by Josephus are not competelyy identical (*Antt.* XVIII, 341: See; XVIII, 26: Sethi or Seth).

21. For equivalents to the name Caiaphas in the rabbinic texts (nowhere can it be identified certainly) and the difficulty of reading it in the inscription of ossuary 6 of the Herodian period, discovered with others during the creation of the 'Peace Forest' in Jerusalem, see the thorough study by E.Puech, 'A-t-on redécouvert le tombeau du grand prêtre Caïphe?', *MondeB* 80, 1993, 42–7. The author's reply to the question posed in the title is that 'neither philology nor phonetics nor onomastics nor the archaeological and anthropological remains are in favour of such an identification'.

22. For the attitude of this line, which is very much open to criticism, see above, 16. The texts have been collected in [Strack-]Billerbeck II, 568–71. See also P.Gaechter, 'The Hatred of the House of Annas', *TS* 8, 1947, 3–34 = *Petrus und seine Zeit*, Innsbruck 1958, 67–104. The fact that the high priest's ceremonial garment was kept under seal in the

Antonia (having suffered an identical fate under the Herods) down to the government of Vitellius, successor of Pilate, and the deposition of Caiaphas in 37 by the same Vitellius confirms the grip the Roman authorities had on the local Jewish government.

23. Blinzler (*The Trial of Jesus*, 83) has noted this (despite the title of the chapter).

24. C.Kopp (*Itinéraires*, 652 n.277) writes: 'During the thirteenth century, Annas's house was pointed out at the beginning of the Via Dolorosa, and from the fourteenth century to our day, at the convent of Armenian nuns, *Dêr esêtûni*, at the gate of Zion, east of the Armenian Patriarchate.'

25. This question in fact goes beyond our concerns. See Kopp, *Itinéraires*, 560–6.

26. See above, 11.

27. See the detailed examination of this passage in Légasse, 'Jésus devant le sanhédrin', 192–4.

28. 'Jésus devant le sanhédrin', 293–4. A relevant bibliography will be found in this article.

29. Benoit confirms this meaning on the basis of the other passages in the Gospel where the expression appears (Matt.12.14; 22.15; 27.7; 28.12; Mark 3.6), 'in which the adjunct participles *exelthontes, poreuthentes, synachthentes* indicate . . . clearly the act of meeting to deliberate' (294). But it has to be noted that these participles are lacking in Mark 15.1 and Matt.17.1 in particular, which is by no means an insignificant fact; if there was deliberation, it is not said in the two Gospels that the Sanhedrin met again after momentarily dispersing.

30. See Légasse, 'Jésus devant le sanhédrin', 195f.

31. It is not necessary to suppose that Luke had particular information about this or even saw that a nocturnal trial was illegal. Here, rather, we have something that a 'historian' who is concerned to be credible feels convenient. The parallel notes in Acts (4.3, 5; 5.21; 22.30) confirm this; here we see the Sanhedrin also sitting in the morning to judge the apostles.

32. Bultmann, *History*, 270, 272.

33. For the place in question see above, 49f.

34. In Mark 14.54,66, the word *aulê* is better understood in the sense of 'palace', not 'court', since the former sense is evident in 15.16, where *aulê* is synonymous with praetorium. See also 100 n.43. There is no point in imagining a change of place in Luke between 22.54 and 22.66, contrary to the suggestion of Blinzler, *The Trial of Jesus*, 115–16.

35. See Sanhedrin 4.1. See also b.Megillah 14a. Acording to Sherwin White *(Roman Society*, 45), the Jewish authorities were in a hurry because of the festival: so they had good reasons for holding an unusual nocturnal session in order to be able to bring the affair to Pilate at a good moment (see above, 75). The author adds, in support of such a session: 'Why light a fire . . . when everyone is sleeping . . .?' But quite apart from the fact that this latter detail also appears in John, who does not mention any session of the Sanhedrin, such expedients are useless the moment the historical consistency of the nocturnal session disappears after an internal criticism of the Synoptic Gospels and a comparison of them with John. Among attempts to salvage the nocturnal session of the Sanhedrin, reference could be made to the thesis put forward by Cohn *(Trial*, 94–141). According to this author, who is a judge at the Supreme Court of Israel, Jesus was arrested on the orders of the Romans and they prescribed, or perhaps better authorized, a 'preliminary enquiry'; in fact this was not carried out by the Sanhedrin but simply by the high priest along with some assistants. The possible initiative of the Jewish authorities would stem from a desire to 'save Jesus', not because of an interest in his person but for purely political reasons, because of his popularity. Since Jesus refused to co-operate and pleaded not guilty, the session could only end with one conclusion: he had to die. This theory, like many others of the same kind, mixes a critical use of the Gospels with a good deal of arbitrariness. In particular, recourse to the 'preliminary enquiry' has no foundation, either in the texts of the New Testament (in particular, the example from Acts 22.30, where the tribune makes Paul appear before the Sanhedrin, is of more than doubtful historicity) or in Jewish or Roman usage. As we have seen earlier, the arrest of Jesus was a matter for the Jewish hierocracy and only for them.

36. See above, 43.

37. One might add that, according to the Bible, to spit in someone's face is a sign of profound scorn (Num.12.14; Deut.25.9; Job 20.10). But the symbol is widespread in antiquity: for example, Seneca (*Ad Helviam*, 13.7) reports that an Athenian spat in Aristides' face as he was led away to execution.

38. One might also think of the police who arrested Jesus and then led him to Annas, who are also called *hypêretai* in John 18.3, 12, 18 (see also 19.6; Acts 5.22, 26). But the context in Mark, who mentions a 'servant girl' (14.66,69), points more towards the domestic staff of Annas, though that does not mean that we can exclude the involvement of the guards.

39. Whether or not the evangelist was thinking of the 'disciple whom

Jesus loved', the question of the historicity of the presence and the role of this figure and the circumstances remains. It is difficult to see a follower of Jesus on familiar terms with the worst enemies of his master. Dodd (*Tradition*, 86) notes in this connection that 'this vivid narrative, every step of which is clear and convincing, is either the product of a remarkable dramatic *flair* or it rests on superior information'. So, will not the anonymous disciple be 'merely a *dramatis personae* created to provide a plausible means of getting Peter inside'? The question whether the woman on the gate with whom the disciple chats is a figure borrowed from the story of Peter's denial, a dramatized episode in which the provocators are themselves hardly more than '*dramatis personae*', is equally pertinent.

40. However, the motivation provided in Matt.26.58 comes only from the evangelist.

41. Initially Peter's denial has no connection with the word of Jesus in Luke 22.31–32, in which the phrase 'when you return' is additional and provides the link with the announcement of the denial in vv.33–34, verses which are derived from Mark 14.29–31. Reduced to its primitive form in this way, what is said in Luke 22.31–32 relates to the persecution of the future community, and it is the faithfulness of Peter which is guaranteed by Jesus' prayer: see Linnemann, *Studien*, 72–7.

42. Matthew anticipates this setting in more precise terms during the conspiracy, which is thought to take place in the 'palace' (*aulê*) of the high priest (26.3, influenced by Mark 14.54 par. Matt.26.58: *aulê*).

43. For the ancient rampart of Jerusalem see Josephus, *BJ* V, 144. – The bridge, rediscovered in 1838, is known as 'Robinson's Arch'. For the council room see Josephus, *BJ* VI, 354.

44. Middot 5.4; Sanhedrin 11.2; see also Pea 2.6; Eduyyot 7.4; Tamid 2.5.

45. In the Septuagint (I Chron 22.2; Amos 5.11) the word *ghazit* ('cut stones') is translated as *xystos*.

46. On the other hand we must regard as fantasy the information in the Gemara (b.Aboda Zara, 8b, etc., see [Strack-]Billerbeck I, 100) which states that forty years after the destruction of the temple the Sanhedrin left the *lishkat ha-gazît* (or was expelled from it) and thenceforth met in the bazaar(s) (*hanût, hanuyyôt*), which some scholars identify with the shops on the temple mount, even on the Mount of Olives (see above, 125 n.15). Jeremias (*Jerusalem*, 49) notes that this transfer 'is evidently an illustration of the withdrawal of the right of capital punishment'.

47. One pointer in this direction could be that Jesus was crucified with other victims (see above, 91f.). However, it would be necessary to prove that these had been arrested on the orders of the Jewish authorities before having been brought before the governor, which is not feasible.

48. See Sanhedrin 4.1; cf. 70–74 above.

5. The Roman Trial

1. A distinction here between 'declaration of guilt' and 'formal verdict' (thus Benoit, *RB* 68, 1961, 596 n.3 = id., *Exégèse et théologie* III, Paris 1968, 256 n.1) is a play on words.

2. See Tacitus, *Annals* XV, 44. See also above 2f.

3. See above, 88–90.

4. See the survey of opinions in Blinzler, *The Trial of Jesus*, 157–63; Léon-Dufour, 'Passion', 1486–7.

5. They mainly derive from Müller, 'Möglichkeit'.

6. We should remember that the Roman provinces of the imperial period were divided into senatorial provinces ruled by a proconsul under the authority of the senate and imperial provinces (large military districts) governed by a legate directly answerable to the emperor; finally, the least important provinces were governed by a prefect or procurator (see n.7), also under the direct authority of the emperor. However, in the case of Judaea the legate of Syria, head of the main Roman army in the East, in the last resort had the responsibility for maintaining order in this province.

7. It now seems that the title 'procurator' (Greek *epitropos*) became the usage only under Claudius, in 46 CE (if this is the case, the title is wrongly given to Pilate by Tacitus in the passage quoted; see Dodd, *Tradition*, 96 n.1). Previously he was called 'prefect' (*praefectus, eparchos*). The word *hêgemôn* (*praeses*) is used to denote the same figure throughout the New Testament (but note *eparcheia* in Acts 23.3, 34; 25.1) and once in Josephus (*Antt.* XVIII 25), who applies it to Gessius Florus. For the question see especially Lémonon, *Pilate*, 43–58.

8. The theory of Lietzmann, 'The Trial of Jesus'. Winter, *Trial*, takes the same line. The two authors have drawn their arguments from Juster (*Juifs*, II, 127–45), according to whom the Sanhedrin, under the procurators, 'could inflict all the penalties prescribed by the Jewish law, including the different sorts of capital punishment, and carry them out itself' (133).

9. See the texts in Juster, *Juifs* II, 138 n.1. This testimony contradicts

that given elsewhere in the same literature, according to which this right was suppressed forty years before the destruction of the temple (see ibid., and 133 n.1). We shall return to the topic later.

10. For more details see Lémonon, *Pilate,* 72–97; Müller, 'Möglichkeit'.

11. *Antt.* XX, 197–203. Agrippa II, inheriting the privileges of his uncle and predecessor Herod of Chalcis, had charge of the temple and the right to nominate the high priests (Josephus, *BJ* II, 223; *Antt.* XX, 104, 222).

12. Catchpole, 'Problem', 61.

13. Lémonon, *Pilate,* 91.

14. Josephus, *BJ* VI, 300–9.

15. The man posed less political danger than Jesus of Nazareth, since he did not have disciples, as the latter did.

16. These texts are quoted and commented on in detail by Lémonon, *Pilate,* 81–90.

17. See Légasse, *Stephanos,* 207–210.

18. M.Sanhedrin 7,2. For more details see Le Moyne, *Les Sadducéens,* 236–8; Lémonon, *Pilate,* 93–4. For the date see especially the argument by Jeremias, 'Geschichtlichkeit', 146.

19. Philo, *Leg. ad Caium,* 212; Josephus, *BJ* VI, 126.

20. *Antt.* XV, 417.

21. See the references in Lémonon, *Pilate,* 93; A.Pelletier, *Philon, 'Legatio ad Caium',* OPhA 32, Paris 1962, 217 n.7.

22. Müller, 'Möglichkeit', 67–9.

23. Sherwin White (*Roman Society,* 38; 'Trial', 109) is wrong in thinking that the Sanhedrin was authorized to have Gentiles, even Roman citizens, who had been caught violating the sanctuary, executed. The quotation is from Lémonon, *Pilate,* 93. The case of Paul, according to Acts 21.27–36, is to be excluded here: although he was suspected of having introduced a Gentile into the temple, Paul was a Jew.

24. Winter, *Trial,* 109. The distinction between religious crime and civil crime exploited by E.Stauffer (*Jerusalem und Rom,* Dtb 331, Bern 1957, 121) to attribute to the Sanhedrin competence only over the first is in reality untenable, since it was easy for a jurisdiction jealous of its rights to give a civil trial a religious colouring; see Gnilka, 'Der Prozess Jesu', 29.

25. Mark 15.2–15; Matt.27.11–26; Luke 23.2–5; John 18.28–19.16. The fact is also recalled in Acts 3.13; 4.27; 13.28; I Tim.6.13.

26. The 'You say [it]' in Mark 15.2 is an affirmation, but a calculated one.

27. This does not mean that we have to follow G.Braumann ('Markus 15,2–5 und Markus 14, 55–64', *ZNW* 52, 1961, 273–8) in regarding the second narrative as fabrication pure and simple on the basis of the first, since the differences between the two are too considerable. To explain their similarity it is enough to see them as the work of the same author.

28. For Luke 23.1–2, 4–5 see the discussion in Fitzmyer, *Luke* II, 1472. The author brings out numerous traces of Lukan redaction in these verses. For Luke 23.2 and in the same sense see Schneider, 'Political Charge'; Radl, 'Sonderüberlieferung', 132–4.

29. Including in John, where nothing in fact prepares for Pilate's question in 18.33 (the presentation of Jesus as a simple 'malefactor' in 18.30 cannot perform this function).

30. We find the pendant to this in connection with Paul, in Acts 17.6–9, for the same apologetic purpose. See also above, 67.

31. See Deut.21.6–9; Ps.26.6; 73.13. Origen (*Comm. in Matt.*, GCS 38, 259) noted that washing the hands corresponds to Jewish, and not Roman, usage. In particular for the dream as a means of revelation see Matt.1.20; 2.12, 13, 19, 22.

32. See Légasse, 'Jésus roi'.

32. Jean Colin, *Les Villes libres de l'Orient gréco-romain et l'envoi au supplice par acclamations populaires*, Lat 82, Brussels and Berchem 1965. See the criticism of this work by P.Benoit, *RB* 78, 1971, 137–8; Lémonon, *Pilate*, 96–7.

34. Thus in the affair of the standards (*BJ* II, 169–74; *Antt.* XVIII, 55–9) and the incident provoked by the construction of an aqueduct (*BJ* II, 175–7; *Antt.* XVIII, 60–2).

35. See above, 34f. The popular reversal of feelings from the ovation with the palms, often exploited in Christian preaching, has little chance of having roots in history if one accepts, as we have done, that the demonstration held on Jesus' arrival in Jerusalem was not as large as the Gospels suggest, see above, 26.

36. In Mark (15.11, 14), this declaration is addressed to the crowd, while the accusations in Mark 15.3 are made only by the high priests. In 23.4a Luke adds the crowd to the high priests, to put here a first verdict of 'not guilty'.

37. It can be found in Vanel, 'Prétoire', 513–21.

38. See the bibliography in Blinzler, *The Trial of Jesus*, 173–6. For a

systematic presentation of the argument that this was Herod's palace see
Benoit, 'Prétoire'; Vanel, 'Prétoire', 521–54.

39. For Philo, compare *Leg.ad Caium* 306 (*en oikiai tôn epitropôn*)
and 299 (*en tois . . . Hêrôdou basileiois*). In Josephus, see *BJ* II, 301. In
the interval following the death of Herod the Great (4 BCE), Sabinus
already installed himself in this palace: *BJ* II, 44; *Antt.* XVIII, 255. For
the word *aulê* see above, 134, n.34. For the name Gabbatha see Dalman
(*Jesus-Jeshua*, 13), who hesitates between *gabbetâ*, 'hunch', and *gab-
bahtâ*, 'bald forehead' (thus in Dalman, *Grammatik*, 160), excluding
gabbetâ meaning 'bowl'. Today specialists tend to prefer the first term, in
the sense indicated. See among others [Strack-]Billerbeck II, 572;
L.H.Vincent, 'Le Lithostrotos évangélique', *RB* 59, 1952, 512–30: 524.

40. Benoit ('Prétoire', 534 = 319), where there is a relevant
bibliography.

41. See the photograph in *RB* 42, 1933, pl.viii, 1. Note the remarks
by Benoit ('Prétoire', 548 = 336 nn.2 or 3) on the drawings of games
engraved on the paving stones of the Antonia. In fact they do not bear
the slightest relationship to the scene of the insults described in the
Gospels. See also the documentation in Benoit, 'Prétoire', 545–7 =
333–5. The author shows that alongside the specialized sense of
'pavement in marquetry or mosaic', the etymological sense of simple
'stone pavement' is still maintained for *lithostroton*. See finally L.H.Vin-
cent, 'L'Antonia et le Prétoire', *RB* 42, 1933, 83–113: 104.

42. *BJ* V, 176–82. For the possible location in relation to the present
city see Kopp, *Itinéraires*, 575.

43. The word *aulê* here clearly has this sense; see above, 134 n.34.
The sense of 'palace' predominates in Josephus, particularly in connection with Herod's palace (*BJ* II, 312, 318, 429, 441, 530, 557; V, 176;
VI, 358, 376; *Life* 46, 407). But the sense of 'courtyard' is equally
attested in his writings (*BJ* V, 227; VIII, 241 ,etc.).

44. *BJ* II, 301–8. See also above, 78.

45. For the title see above, 137 n.7.

46. Lémonon, *Pilate*, 125–6.

47. According to Philo (*Leg. ad Caium*, 302–3), a report to the
emperor on Pilate's administration is said to have mentioned 'the
briberies, the insults, the robberies, the outrages and wanton injuries,
the execution without trial constantly repeated, the ceaseless and
supremely grievous cruelty'. For the notably different picture in the
Synoptics, which differs from that of the Fourth Gospel, see Légasse,
'Jésus roi', 146–57.

48. Was the Tiberium a temple? A monument? An administrative building? For the inscription in Caesarea, a useful epigraphic testimony to Pilate's presence in Judaea, and its interpretation, see Lémonon, *Pilate*, 23–32; 'L'Inscription de Pilate', *MondeB* 56, 1988, 33. Only Pilate's predecessor, Valerius Gratus, who was in charge for eleven years (15–26), can be compared with him. None of the other governors apart from Felix (52–59/60) lasted longer than five years, and the majority of them occupied the post for only two years.

50. See Cicero, *De legibus* 3.8: '*Salus populi suprema lex esto.*' For the rights and prerogatives of the function of the prefect, especially in judicial matters, see Mommsen, *Strafrecht* I, 266–92; H.G.Pflaum, *Essai sur les procurateurs équestres sous le Haut-Empire*, Paris 1949–1950; F.-M.Abel, *Histoire de la Palestine depuis la conquête d'Alexandre jusqu'à l'invasion arabe* I, EtB, Paris 1952, 426–32; H.Last, 'Coercitio', *RAC* III, 235–43; Sherwin-White, *Roman Society*, 1–23; Schürer, *History* I, 367–70.

50. The technical term for provincial judgments was 'judgments *extra ordinem*'.

51. Sherwin-White, 'Trial', 100.

52. It is impossible to establish how much Greek Jesus knew. For this question see A.W.Argyle, 'Did Jesus Speak Greek?', *ExpT* 67, 1955–56, 92–3, 383; id., 'Greek Among the Jews of Palestine in New Testament Times', *NTS* 20, 1973–74, 87–9; J.N.Sevenster, '*Do You Know Greek?' How Much Greek Could the First Jewish-Christians Have Known?*, NT.S 19, Leiden 1968; A. Díez Macho, *La lengua hablada por Jesucristo*, Madrid 1976, 65–78.

53. The response of the Jews, 'Were he not a malefactor we would not have handed him over to you' (John 18.30), is vague. It is only towards the end of the session (19.12) that we find the accusation that Jesus claimed the throne, again only in an indirect form.

54. See above, 57.

55. Nothing is gained by conjecturing, with T.A.Mohr *(Markus- und Johannespassion*, AThANT 70, Zurich 1982, 286), an inversion by the evangelist of Mark 15.2 and 15.3, the original order of which is said to have been compromising in the eyes of the empire because it put the affirmative response of Jesus after the accusations of the high priests. In fact: 1. there is no evidence of the presence of another version of the accusation in the source of Mark; 2. what we read in 15.3 is vague and does not prepare for the question; 3. the accusations of v.3 and Pilate's second question (v.4) are inseparable; 4. John 18.30 is no help here,

since it does not attest an accusation which would have been capable of prompting Pilate's question: this is as abrupt in John as in Mark and Matthew.

56. Josephus, *Antt.* XVII, 285.

57. Josephus, *Antt.* XVII, 272.

58. Ibid., 273–7.

59. Id., *BJ* II, 60–2; see also *Antt.* 278–84.

60. Josephus, *BJ* II, 439–440, 443–8. See Hengel, *Zealots,* 362–6. From this perspective the son differed from the father, since Judas the Galilean defended an absolute theocracy; see Josephus, *BJ* II, 118, 433; *Antt.* XVIII, 73, and Hengel, ibid., 107–10.

61. See 57f. above.

62. The term 'Jew' derives from a usage alien to the people themselves (but for the title see below, 157f. n.86). In Graeco-Roman vocabulary it denote Israelites where they are and not just the Israelite population of 'Judaea'. It is best to avoid speaking here of *perduellio.* In reacting against Mommsen's too inclusive classification (*Strafgericht* II, 243–93), Brecht (*Perduellio,* especially 1–14, 120–5, 261–5) has emphasized that under the republic the notion of *perduellio* is generally supplanted by that of *crimen maiestatis,* despite Ulpian (*Dig.,* 48, 4, 11), who groups what also relates to the crime of *lèse-majesté* under the term *perduellio:* '*Perduellionis reus, hostili animo adversus rem publicam vel principem animatus*' (he is guilty of *perduellio* who nurtures a hostile design on public affairs or the prince').

63. See Müller, 'Möglichkeit', 73–8. See also above, 54.

64. Apart from the designation of the high priests, which made them really puppets in the hands of the Roman power, the way in which the priestly vesture was kept in the Antonia, at least until 45 CE, was the height of a policy which revolted Jewish piety. See Jeremias, *Jerusalem,* 148–9.

65. Hegesippus, in Eusebius, *HE* III, 20, 1–5. For this note and its legendary nature see G.Lüdemann, *Opposition to Paul in Jewish Christianity,* Minneapolis 1989, 120–3; R.Bauckham, *Jude and the Relatives of Jesus in the Early Church,* Edinburgh 1990, 94–106.

66. A survey of this can be found in Fitzmyer, *Luke* II, 1478–9.

67. Josephus (*Antt.* XVIII, 122) relates that Antipas accompanied Vitellius, legate of Syria, to Jerusalem on the occasion of a festival. Although as a Galilean Jesus was under the jurisdiction of Antipas, since the crime was thought to have been committed in Jerusalem, Pilate had full power to judge it (*forum delicti*). Moreover, as Sherwin-White

(*Roman Society*, 28–9), notes, 'one does not expect a governor in the late Republic and early Principate, when faced by a malefactor, to bother about the very fine question whether his *imperium* allowed him to deal with a man who was *in* his province but not *of* his province.' Hoehner (*Herod Antipas*, 236–7), who regards the mediation with Antipas as historic, suggests that Pilate was making a diplomatic gesture towards Antipas, who had been disturbed by the massacre of the Galileans in Easter 32 (Luke 13.1) and in the affair of the gilded buckles (Philo, *Leg. ad Caium*, 299–304). A connection with the first fact is also established by Blinzler, 'Die Niedermetzelung von Galiläern durch Pilatus', *NT* 2, 1958, 24–49: 48.n.1.; id., *The Trial of Jesus*, 202.

68. Denaux, 'L'Hypocrisie', 265–8.

69. For details about the terms and expressions see Fitzmyer, *Luke* II, 1479.

70. In favour of the historicity of the Lukan episode Sherwin-White (*Roman Society*, 31) cites the privilege accorded to Herod the Great: he was the only king to whom the emperor gave the power to claim the extradition of one of his subjects who had escaped, even to a city which was not under his jurisdiction (Josephus, *BJ* I, 474). Antipas is said to have kept 'some vestige' of this privilege, hence Pilate's sending of Jesus to him. But no document bears any trace of the matter. In excluding the tetrarch from the number of those responsible for the death of Jesus I am not following some apocryphas and some modern authors; see Blinzler, *The Trial of Jesus*, 194–204.

71. See above, 57.

72. See above, 57.

73. Luke 23.17 ('Now he was obliged to release one man to them at a festival') is almost unanimously recognized as a gloss, after Matt.27.15; Mark 15.6. For the Lukanisms in this passage see J.Jeremias, *Die Sprache des Lukasevangeliums*, KEK, Sonderband, Göttingen 1980, 303–4.

74. In Mark 15.6 the 'festival', though it is not specified, is the Passover, as in 14.2 according to 14.1 ('Passover' and 'Unleavened Bread').

75. The terms *stasiastês* and *stasis* are used by Josephus (*BJ* VI, 157; *Antt.* XX, 117) for the rebellion against Rome.

76. To the Gospels must be added Acts 3.14.

77. See Pesahim 8.6. See the criticism of his allegation in Jeremias, *Eucharistic Words*, 73. Blinzler, *The Trial of Jesus*, 207–11, tries in vain to establish that the prisoner in question had been imprisoned by a non-Jewish authority.

78. Livy V, 13,8.

79. See Deissmann, *Light from the Ancient East*, 266–8.

80. See Langdon, 'The Release of the Prisoner at the Passover', *ExpT* 29, 1918, 328–38 (the king releasing a prisoner on the 6th, 16th and 26th of the eighth month). These considerations are taken up in another form by R.L.Merritt, 'Jesus Barabbas and the Paschal Pardon', *JBL* 104, 1985, 57–68. This author, who recalls the freeing of Jehoiakim by Awil-Marduk (II Kings 25.17–30; Jer.52.31–34), suggests that Mark used this ancient usage to give an impression of authenticity to a fictitious account and to present Jesus as realizing the prophecy of Isa.53 in which the 'Servant' takes the punishment of criminals upon himself.

81. Documentation in [Strack]-Billerbeck I, 1031; Fitzmyer, *Luke* II, 1490. Theories according to which Jesus and Barabbas are one and the same, based on a theological or functional translation of the word *Abba*, have been developed by H.A.Rigg, 'Barabbas', *JBL* 64, 1945, 417–56 ('Jesus son of the Father'); H.Z.Maccoby, 'Jesus and Barabbas', *NTS* 16, 1969–70, 55–60 ('Jesus the Teacher'); S.L.Davies, 'Who is Called Bar Abbas?', *NTS* 27, 1980–1981, 160–2 ('Son of Abba' = 'Son of God'). Apart from the fact that *Abba* is well attested as a proper name, the Gospel texts do not offer any basis for these conjectures; Jesus and Barabbas are clearly distinguished in them and there is no suspicion of any Christian manipulation on the basis of the fact that the Jews took the side of Jesus. These theories originate from the Caesarean variant in Matt.27.16, 17 according to which Jesus' rival was called 'Jesus Barabbas'.

82. Compare with the persons mentioned in Mark 15.21, who are equally supposed to be known.

83. Thus again in the affair of the aqueduct: see above, 134 n.34.

84. See above, 91f.

85. The action of the high priests in this instance is particularly inappropriate: it is hard to see these 'collaborators' demanding the freeing of a rebel.

86. To suppose a confession on the part of Jesus which will have made the sentence superfluous (*confessus pro iudicato est*) is pure conjecture. And what will Jesus have confessed to to incur such a punishment? As for the formulation of the sentence, scholars (thus Blinzler, *The Trial of Jesus*, 238 and n.5) sometimes cite examples taken from comedy: Plautus, *Asinaria*, 940, '*I in crucem*'; *Poenulus*, 271, '*abi in malam crucem*'. But that is to forget that these are popular expressions meaning 'Go hang yourself' or 'Go to the devil', and one cannot

guarantee that they imitate a legal formula. Far less can one cite in this connection a phrase from the *Satyricon* ('If the magistrates know it, you will be crucified' [*ibis in crucem*], 137); its context takes us right away from audience chambers. John 19.13 makes Pilate ascend his tribunal only at the end, since in this Gospel the interrogation takes place within the palace. Since here the location is artificial (see above 57f., 62), and given the support of an analogous scene reported by Josephus (*BJ* II, 301–8, see above, 78), we have no reason to envisage an interrogation in the open air which will have been concluded by the sentence pronounced on the *bema*.

6. *Days and Hours*

1. See Blinzler, *The Trial of Jesus*, 72–80.

2. Mark 15.42; Matt.27, 62; Luke 23.54, 56; John 19.31,42.

3. Mark 14.12, 16; Matt.26.17–19; Luke 22.7–15. The Gospel of Peter (II, 5; cf. V,15) also makes Jesus die on the eve of the Passover, and it is followed by other ancient witnesses: see Mara, *Évangile de Pierre*, 82–6. The apocrypha could only serve to confirm the Johannine christology if we could be sure that it was independent of the canonical Gospels, the Fourth Gospel in particular, which is far from being established, see above, 7f.

4. Put forward by Jaubert, *Calendrier biblique*. It has been taken up and completed systematically by Ruckstuhl, *Chronologie,* and his articles mentioned in the bibliography. There is a list of those for and those against in Blinzler, *The Trial of Jesus*, 78–80.

5. See especially the criticisms of P.Benoit, *RB* 65, 1968, 590–4 = *Exégèse et théologie* I, Paris 1961, 255–61 (on Jaubert); *RB* 72, 1965, 453–4 (on Ruckstuhl).

6. Josephus (*Antt.* XVIII, 19) does not offer any supporting proof in indicating that the Essenes who barred themselves from the common sanctuary performed their sacrifices separately (*aph'auton*).

7. See Jeremias, *Eucharistic Words*, 40–41, especially the conclusions on 41.

8. For a detailed demonstration see ibid., 41–84.

9. This point could be confirmed by the Fourth Gospel, according to which the Last Supper also took place in Jerusalem and in which Judas departs by night (13.30). However, in connection with this latter feature it is going far to see a trace of the Synoptic chronology here, given the symbolism attached to darkness in John. The other traces of this

chronology are even less evident. Thus for John 13.29 (cf. Jeremias, *Eucharistic Words*, 53–4; Schnackenburg, *Gospel according to John III*, 31–2), or the parenthesis in 19.31 (see below, n.18), not to mention the less tortuous arguments.

10. See below, 147 n.23. In adding, 'This, however, is most unlikely so early in the morning (Mark 15.25)', Jeremias (*Eucharistic Words*, 76) fails to note the artificial aspect of Mark's indications of time (see above, 74).

11. Dalman (*Jesus-Jeshua*, 100–1), to whom Jeremias (ibid.) refers, indicates, among other examples, Gen.24.64; 27.3; Isa.40.6; 55.12 (*sadeh*) and the Targum with, in Gen.3.1; 6.14, *bara* ('outside').

12. See the commentaries of Pesch, *Markusevangelium* II, 319–22; Ernst, *Evangelium nach Markus*, 397–8; Schmithals, *Evangelium nach Markus* II, 588, and the argument in Jeremias (*Eucharistic Words*, 71–3), who is unfortunately allergic to any question about the involvement and the intentions of the evangelist in these verses. In another direction, Schenke (*Studien*, 64–5), followed by Gnilka (*Markus* II, 220), imputes to Mark a concern to show that the plan of the Jewish authorities is not realized, but rather that of God, who foresaw that Jesus would die on the actual feast of Passover. Although it is in conformity with the Markan irony, his exegesis does not meet the needs of the context.

13. For *heortê* see Ps.73.4 LXX; John 7.11; Epictetus, *Syllogisms* I, 12; Plotinus, *Enneads*, VI, 6,12. The words *en dolo* apply to the whole enterprise, from the arrest to the murder.

14. Jeremias, *Eucharistic Words*, 76. For the doubtful value of the Talmudic note in b.Sanhedrin 43a as confirmation of the chronology of the Fourth Gospel see above, 6.

15. These texts, that of Paul in particular, only confirm that the Johannine chronology is of a purely typological and theological kind. Far less can one claim I Cor.15.20 for the same view, seeing the word *aparche* as an allusion to the offering of the 'firstfruits' on 16 Nisan, since the word is used here in a figurative sense. For the whole passage see Jeremias, *Eucharistic Words*, 74 (the paschal interpretation of the death of Jesus derives from his own words at the Last Supper).

16. Ex.12.10 LXX; 12.46; Num.9.12.

17. John 11.55; see also 2.13; 6.4.

18. We cannot identify a vestige of the Synoptic chronology in John 19.31, contrary to [Strack-]Billerbeck II, 581–2; Bultmann, *John*, 676 n.6; Jeremias, *Eucharistic Words*, 80–1; Barrett, *John*, 461–2. These authors are thinking here or the day of offering the first sheaf ('Omer', Lev.23.11), the day after the Passover, or 16 Nisan. This insinuation

that the 'great day' was the sabbath in question does not have the slightest support in Jewish language, and moreover John (7.37) uses the same expression in connection with the last day of the Feast of Tabernacles.

19. See the survey by Blinzler, *The Trial of Jesus*, 265–70. His proposal on the basis of an alleged gloss in Mark 15.33 has as little basis as the others.

20. Schenk, *Passionsbericht*, 37–9; Gnilka, *Markus* II, 317. These authors refer to Dan.7.12; IV Ezra 4.36–37,42; 13.58.

21. For opinions to this effect see Neirynck, '*Anateilantos tou hêliou*', 100–3 or 211–14.

22. See K.Hruby, 'Les Heures de la prière dans le judaïsme à l'époque de Jésus', in Mgr Cassien and B.Botte (eds.), *La Prière des heures*, LO 35, Paris 1963, 59–84.

23. *Apostolic Tradition* 41 distributes Christian prayer over the third, sixth and ninth hours, according to the following moments of the passion: crucifixion, darkness, piercing. The evident reminiscence of Mark 15.25, 33, 34 is mixed here with a borrowing from John 19.34, and the Johannine scene of the piercing opportunely takes the place of the cry of abandonment in Mark 15.34.

24. The precision of Mark is typical of his redaction, with the two successive adverbs *euthus* and *prôi*. Seneca *(De ira* II, 7,3) evokes 'those thousands of people who run to the forum at dawn' (*prima luce*); Macrobius, *Sat*.I.3: 'The magistrates, after midnight, take the auspices and when the sun rises [*post exortum solem*] move on to business'; Suetonius, *Vespasian* 21: Vespasian did not wait for day to get up and read correspondence and reports; Martial, VIII, 67, 3: at ten in the morning the tribunals stop sitting; Pliny the Elder, Prefect of the Fleet, finished his working day at ten or eleven in the morning (Pliny, *Ep*.III.5,9,11; VI.16, 4–6). See also Sherwin-White, *Roman Society*, 45; id., 'Trial', 114–15.

7. *The Execution*

1. For a bibliography see Schürer, *History* I, 362–7.
2. See above, 27.
3. The aim here is to harmonize John and the Synoptics at any price. Thus in Blinzler, *The Trial of Jesus*, 223–6, 233–5.
4. See above, 57.
5. Josephus, *BJ* II, 306; V, 449; VII, 200,202; Livy XXXIII 36, 3.

Equally before hanging (Josephus, *BJ* VII, 154), and before being burned (*BJ* VII, 450) or decapitated (*Acts of Justin and his Companions*, 5: H.Musurillo, *The Acts of Christian Martyrs*, OECT, 1972, 46 and 50).

6. Sherwin-White, *Roman Society*, 27.

7. See P.W.Walaskay, 'The Trial and Death of Jesus in the Gospel of John', *JBL* 94, 1975, 81–93: 90–1, with relevant bibliography.

8. A description can be read in Blinzler, *The Trial of Jesus*, 222–3; Leclercq ('Flagellation [Supplice de la]', *DACL* V/2, 1638–48) provides a bibliography with reproductions of the instruments used in this torture.

9. See above, 61.

10. *BJ* II, 301–8.

11. See above, 60f.

12. The reed will have exchanged its role of sceptre for that of an instrument for whipping. Matthew (27.29) restores the objects. For the cruelties suffered by Jesus from the servants of the high priest see above 48f. The combination must derive from Mark, unless John, who reproduces it (19.3, the thorns!), is independent of his predecessor here.

13. Mark (15.17) speaks of 'purple', royal adornment, which Matthew (27.28) corrects into 'scarlet cloak', thinking that such precious material was inappropriate in this military framework. Here the commentators think either of the *sagum* worn by lictors outside Rome or the simple red cloak of soldiers.

14. In summoning 'the *whole* cohort' to the rescue, the evangelists Mark and Matthew exaggerate (compare John 18.3; Acts 23.3), failing to recognize that this cohort was stationed in the Antonia barracks, and not at the praetorium.

15. See above, 65 and 92–4.

16. For the festival of the Sacaea see Dio Chrysostom IV, 67: 'They take one of their prisoners who has been condemned to death, sit him on the royal throne, dress him in the royal adornment, allow him to give orders, to drink and to celebrate marriage, to frolic with the royal concubines during these days [of the festival]; and no one stops him from doing whatever he wants. But when these days are past, they strip him of his clothing, scourge him and hang him.' Strabo (IX, 8,4–5), describing the supposed origin of the Sacaea, says nothing about the episode in question. Berosius (in Athenaeus XIV, 44, 646c) locates it, with the Sacaea of his time, in Babylon. For this custom, its origins and affinities, see J.G.Frazer, *The Golden Bough*, abridged edition London 1922,

274–83, 283–9. For the Saturnalia, Tacitus (*Annals* XIII, 15) reports in the preamble to the assassination of Britannicus that a dice game gave the crown to Nero, and he used his role to humiliate Britannicus. See L.Parmentier, 'Le Roi des saturnales', *RPh* 21, 1897, 143–9 with the observations of F.Cumont, 149–53. A bibliography on this question was assembled by Arndt-Gingrich-Bauer, *Lexicon*, 774, s.v. *Stephanos*. This bibliography disappeared in the sixth edition ed. by K. and B.Aland. For a possible relationship with the festival of the Sacaea, Robbins ('Context-ualization', 1173–4) has emphasized the difference between this alleged model and the episode in the Gospel, while seeing the passion of Jesus as a Christian version of a pattern which was going the rounds. In fact the distance between the two is too great, and the royal claim attributed to Jesus is enough to explain the form taken by the derision.

17. *In Flaccum* 36–71.

18. *Marin* is an Aramaic dialect form, the equivalent of *Maran* ('Our Lord', see I Cor.16.22). Syria is to be taken in the broader sense, as denoting Palestine (see *Letter of Aristeas* 11, 12, 22).

19. For those questioning whether this detail is historical, we should recall that Herod's palace included gardens: Josephus, *BJ* V, 180–1.

20. This took place in summer 38.

21. For the fact that the condemned man himself bore the instrument of his punishment see Artemidorus, *Onirocritica* II, 56: 'The one who has to be nailed (*proselousthai*) to the cross begins by carrying it'; Plutarch, *Instances of Divine Justice*: 'In corporal punishment each of the malefactors bears his own cross'; Gen.rabba 56,3 (36c): '"And Abraham took the wood of the holocaust and put it on his son Isaac", like the one who bears his cross (*selubo*) on his shoulders'; Pesikta rabbati 31.2 (143b): 'And Isaac bore the wood like a man carrying his cross' (*selub shello*). See also below. The announcement *post eventum* of the martyrdom of Peter in John 21.18 seems to indicate that the condemned man was dragged by ropes: see the survey in Brown, *John* II, 1107–8. For the *patibulum* see Plautus, *Carbonaria*, frag.48: 'Let him carry his *patibulum* through the city, then let him be nailed to the cross'; Mostellaria 56–7: 'He will lead you through the street, the *patibulum* across your neck, prodding you with goads'. See also below, 153 n.47. For the *stipes crucis* see also below 156 n.75.

22. See John 10.17–18; 18.40–48; 19.30. For the requisitioning Mark (15.21) and Matthew (27.32) here have the technical verb *aggareuein*. Luke (23.26) substitutes for it *epilambansesthai* (take), a verb which is predominantly Lukan and is better Greek.

23. Josephus, *Antt.* XIV, 115; II Macc.2.24. Jeremias (*Eucharistic Words,* 77), expresses doubts as to whether Simon was a Jew: 'This is nowhere suggested. Simon was also a common name among Greeks.' This is one way of resolving the problem of a return to the country on the day of the Passover, according to the Synoptic chronology (see above, 72). The Greek names of Simon's sons could confirm that he was a Gentile. However, on the one hand we know that names of non-Hebrew provenance were common among the Jews of Palestine: two of the Twelve (Andrew and Philip) have Greek names, and the names of all the members of the college of the Seven (granted, they were of Hellenistic Jewish origin or proselytes) are Greek (Acts 6.5). On the other hand all the Simons mentioned in the New Testament other than the one who bears Jesus' cross are Jewish.

24. Despite Acts 6.9 we cannot reduce the synagogues of the groups listed to one: see Légasse, *Stephanos,* 199–200.

25. There is nothing that forces us to identify this Rufus with his homonym in Rom.16.13, thought to reside in Rome, the traditional place of the composition of the Gospel of Mark.

26. But see n.23 above.

27. See N.Avigad, 'A Depository of Inscribed Ossuaries in the Kidron Valley', *IEJ* 12, 1962, 1–12: 9–11.

28. Irenaeus attests (*Adv.haer.*I, 24,4) that the Gnostic Basilides taught that Simon had been crucified in place of Jesus: 'And this is the Simon who, out of ignorance or error, was crucified, having been metamorphosed by him so that he would be taken for Jesus; as for Jesus himself, he took on the features of Simon, and standing there, mocked the Archons. Being in fact an incorporeal power and the intellect of the unengendered Father, he transformed himself as he willed, and that is how he ascended again to the one who had sent him.' Other statements that Jesus only seemed to be crucified, or that the crucifixion was limited to a Jesus distinct from Christ, can be found in Bauer, *Das Leben Jesus im Zeitalter der neutestamentlichen Apokryphen,* Tübingen 1909, 239. Ignatius (*Trall.*10) already attacked those who claimed that Christ had only 'seemed to suffer'. According to the Qur'an (4, 157), Jesus was not crucified but only his 'semblance': see R.Arnaldez, 'Jésus, fils de Marie, prophète d'Islam', *JJC* 13, Paris 1980, 191–205; K-W.Tröger, 'Sie haben ihn nicht getötet . . . Koptische Schriften von Nag Hammadi als Auslegungshintergrund von Sure, 4, 157', *Carl-Schmidt-Kolloquium aus der Martin-Luther-Universität 1988,* Halle 1990, 221–33; summarized in *TD* 38, 1991, 213–18.

29. Gen.23.2; Deut.34.8; Jer.6.26; Amos 8.10; Mark 5.38–39 par.; Acts 9.2; 9.39. See [Strack-]Billerbeck I, 521–3; IV.1, 582–90.

30. M.Sanhedrin 6.6 (see Jer.16.5–17; 22.18–19). J.Schmidt (*Das Evangelium nach Lukas*, RNT, Regensburg ⁴1960, 346) suggests without any real basis that the women in question, instead of weeping over Jesus, 'were not only protesting against his condemnation but also proclaiming, consciously or not, that he was the king of his people'.

31. See above, 60–2.

32. Mark 15.22; Matt.27.33; John 19.17. Luke 23.33 only gives the translation.

33. Quite apart from many other objections (see Jeremias, *Golgotha*, 1–2), the singular in this case cannot be explained unless we accept that the pious fantasy which locates the burial of Adam's skull at Golgotha is well founded (the first known witness to this is [Pseudo?-]Basil of Caesarea [died 379], *Comm.in Is.* 5, 1, 141, *PG* 30, 348).

34. 593,4 (CCh, SL, LXXV, 17). Cyril of Jerusalem (*Baptismal Catecheses*, XIII, 39, PG 33, 820) speaks of 'holy Golgotha which rises above us, remaining visible to this day and showing even now how because of Christ the rocks were then riven'). Epiphanius (*Haer.*46.5, Holl, GCS II, 208–9), though born in Palestine (around 315), was opposed to this identification, but he does not command much confidence, since on the one hand he wants to establish that the place takes its name from Adam's skull which is buried there and not from any topographical configuration; on the other, he expected to find a 'mountain' (*akra*) there.

35. Parrot (*Golgotha*, 49), referring to Vincent and Abel (*Jérusalem nouvelle*, 93). These latter wrote: 'The anthropomorphic specification is also deceptive, though a happy one, when the Palestinian denotes such a place on his coasts as a shoulder (*ketef*), a back (*dahr*) and a belly (*batn*)'.

36. The first is Bishop Melito of Sardes in the middle of the third century, followed by Alexandria of Cappadocia (around 212), Pionius of Smyrna (died 250), Firmilian of Caesarea (between 231 and 250); see the references in Jeremias, *Golgotha*, 20 n.1.

37. Compare 'Gordon's Calvary' and the Garden Tomb; see Vincent, 'Garden Tomb: histoire d'un mythe', *RB* 34, 1926, 201–31; Parrot, *Golgotha*, 59–65.

38. See Eusebius of Caesarea, *Life of Constantine* III, 25–8; Heikel, GCS I, pp.88–91.

39. For the archaeology of the Anastasis or the Holy Sepulchre see above all V.Corbo, *Il Santo Sepolcro di Gerusalemme. Aspetti*

archeologici dalle origini al periodo crociato (3 vols), Jerusalem 1982. See also id., 'Il santo Sepolcro di Gerusalemme', *La Terre Santa, Studi di Archeologia. Atti del simposio 'Trent'anni di Archeologia in Terra Santa', Roma, 27–30 aprile 1982*, BPAA 23, Rome 1983, 123–7; 'Il Santo Sepolcro di Gerusalemme: nova et vetera', *SBFLA* 28, 1988, 391–422. See also *Monde B* 33, 1984.

40. *BJ* V, 146: 'The second wall started from the gate of the first wall called Gennath and, surrounding only the north quarter of the city, went up to the Antonia.' There are other allusions to this same rampart in *BJ* V, 303, 331, 342 and indirectly, V, 158.

41. John 19.17, with *exêlthen*, does not clearly imply an exit from the city. On the other hand, from the fact that it changes the expression 'outside the camp' (*exo tês parembolês*) of the texts of the Pentateuch (see below) to 'outside the gate' (*exo tês pylês*), Heb.13.12 puts the crucifixion of Jesus outside the city. There is the same testimony to the killing of Stephen, who is taken 'outside the city' (*exo tês poleôs*) to be stoned. For the Jewish law see Lev.24.14; 15.36. According to a *baraita* (b.Sanhedrin, 42b), the stoning should have taken place outside the 'three camps', the first being the inner court of the temple, the second the temple mount and the third Jerusalem: see J.Schachter, *Hebrew-English Edition of the Babylonian Talmud. Sanhedrin*, London ²1969, 42b, a, n.6. For Roman usages see Plautus, *Miles gloriosus*, 358–9: 'Here you are, I think, in the posture in which you will soon have to die at the gate of the city (*extra portam*), your arms outstretched on the gibbet.' The practice of leaving the corpses of those who had been crucified to decompose on the crosses (see above, 97) called for a place sufficiently far removed from the city.

42. See above, n.40.

43. For this subject and a hypothesis about the position of the 'second wall' see U.Lux, 'Vorläufiger Bericht über die Ausgrabung unter der Erlöserkirche im Muristan in der Altstadt von Jerusalem in den Jahren 1970 und 1971', *ZDPV* 88, 1972, 185–201, pls. 18–23; K.J.H.Vriezen, 'Zweiter vorläufiger Bericht über die Ausgrabung unter der Erlöserkirche im Muristan in der Altstadt von Jerusalem (1972–1974)', *ZDPV* 94, 1978, 76–81, pls.5–6; B.E.Schein, 'The Second Wall of Jerusalem', *BA* 44, 1981, 21–6.

44. See Storme, 'Les Lieux saints évangéliques ... XII', 72–3. Schein ('The Second Wall of Jerusalem', 24) writes: 'The second or highest level of the quarry to the west, and perhaps access to the deepest part, were evidently where the Church of the Resurrection is situated

today. Golgotha was probably part of the original hill which was worked to produce this second level. This part itself was not touched because of the bad quality of the stone.'

45. Brown, *John* II, 943.

46. Storme, 'Les Lieux saints évangéliques . . . XII', 73.

47. In II Macc.6.10: 'Two women were taken away for having circumcised their children; their children hanging at their breasts, they were dragged publicly through the city and hurled down from the ramparts'; Josephus, *BJ* II, 246: 'As for Celerius, [Caesar] sent him in chains to Jerusalem with orders to deliver him over to the insults of the Jews and then, when he had been dragged through the city, to behead him'; see also Eusebius, *De martyribus Palestinae* 9, PG 20, 1493, and 149 n.21 above.

48. According to Josephus (*BJ* V, 146), it is here that the 'second wall' began, see above, 152 n.40.

49. Mark 15.23–41 is a composition which came into being in several stages; even the basic stage contained alterations with a view to instructing Christians in the religious significance of the facts related. It seems that they did not form a consecutive narrative, but a series of independent scenes, some derived from the first witnesses, which catechesis will have brought together to reshape them for the purpose indicated.

50. So the reader will not be surprised if I do not discuss here features like the darkness at noon, the rending of the curtain of the temple, the centurion's confession of faith or the resurrection of the dead who return from Sheol through the riven rocks. These details and their purpose belong in a commentary on the Gospels.

51. Dioscurides (*Materia medica* I, 64,3) mentions the stupefying effect of myrrh. As for the mixture, Pliny (*Natural History*, XI 15,19) speaks of wine perfumed with myrrh. However, the *murina* will not have been wine mixed with myrrh but a liqueur wine; see J.André, *Pline l'Ancien, 'Histoire naturelle' XIV*, CUFr, Paris 1958, 122–3.

52. The Talmud (b.Sanhedrin) indicates that the condemned man was given a drink made of wine and incense to dull his senses, according to Prov.31.6: 'Give strong drink to him who is perishing, and wine to those in bitter distress.' And a baraita adds that the women of Jerusalem had the custom of offering a narcotic to those who had been condemned. There are other examples in [Strack-]Billerbeck I, 1037–8.

53. Matthew (27.34) states that Jesus, before refusing, nevertheless 'tastes' the drink to realize the prophecy of Ps.69.22 despite everything.

54. Some scholars see a late addition by Matthew here.

55. An abundant documentation on crucifixion is provided by Hengel, *Crucifixion*, 13–113. For the way in which this punishment was inflicted see also Blinzler, *The Trial of Jesus*, 246–50, 263–5. Whereas Mark (15.24), Luke (23.33) and John (19.18) here use the word *stauroun* in the personal sense (John puts it in a relative clause), Matthew further tones down its importance by using it as a participle, to bring out the 'scriptural' sharing of the garments (27.35). No one minimizes the 'scandal' (I Cor.1.23). Compare 150 n.28 above.

56. For Cicero (*In Verrem* II, 5, 168–9), crucifixion is 'the ultimate punishment' (*summum supplicium*), 'the most cruel and most horrible of punishments' (*crudelissimi taeterrimique supplicii*), 'the worst and last of punishments which is inflicted on slaves' (*servitutis extremo summoque supplicio*). Addressing Verres (ibid., V, 6,2): 'This cross that you had set up for condemned slaves *(damnatis)* you reserved for Roman citizens killed without trial!' Tacitus (*Histories* IV, 11) speaks of *servile supplicum*. Crucifixion as a punishment was abolished in the last years of Constantine, under the influence of Christianity: see Mommsen, *Strafgericht* III, 258.

57. See the documentation in Hengel, *Crucifixion*, 90–105.

58. Josephus, *BJ* I, 97; *Antt.* XIII, 380.

59. See the account of the discussion and the bibliography in Fitzmyer, 'Crucifixion', 498–507.

60. For the strange and probably coded note in the Mishnah (Sanhedrin 6, 5) according to which Simon ben Shetach (around 90 BCE) had seventy or eighty sorceresses hung at Ashkelon, see Hengel, *Crucifixion*, 107.

61. *BJ* II, 75; *Antt.* XVII, 295.

62. *BJ* V, 451.

63. Artemidorus, *Onirocritica* II, 53: *gymnoi . . . staurountai*. The description by Suetonius (Nero, 49: *nudi homines cervicem inseri furcae*) is not about crucifixion but the punishment of the fork, which is distinct from it; see Mommsen, *Strafgericht* III, 258 n.2, citing Isidore of Seville, *Etymologies* V, 27, 34, PL 82, 214, where the distinction is clearly made. It is no problem that Mommsen's description (ibid., 256–7) unduly mixes up the two forms of punishment.

64. Those condemned to stoning were wrapped in a linen cloth, men in front, women in front and behind: M.Sanhedrin 6.3.

65. 10.1: '*expoliaverunt eum uestimento eius, et precinxerunt eum lintheo*', in H.C.Kim (ed.), *The Gospel of Nicodemus*, Toronto 1973, 24.

66. For the different models of ancient nails see H.Leclerq, 'Clou', *DACL* III/2, cols 2034–6 (illustrations).

67. The redeeming blood is everywhere associated with the death of Jesus on the cross; this is expressed in brief in Col.1.20, which speaks of the 'blood of his cross' (the reference is less certain in Col.2.14, which is sometimes seen as an allusion to the *titulus*). For the earliest patristic testimony to Jesus having been fixed to the cross by nails see Blinzler, *The Trial of Jesus*, 214–15. Tertullian (*Adv.Marcionem* III, 19,6, CCh, SL, I, 524: '*Solus a populo tam insigniter crucifixus est*') introduced the error that Jesus will have been crucified not only with ropes but also with nails, as a refinement of the torture. Christian art has often represented the two 'thieves' attached to their crosses by ropes, unlike Jesus and to make him more prominent.

68. See Artemidorus, *Onirocritica* II, 56 (see above, 149 n.21); II 53: 'the cross is made of wood and nails like a ship.' Other examples in Holzmeister, '*Crux Domini*', 9–10. See Josephus *BJ* II, 308; V, 451 (see 90 above). For the shedding of blood see *Antt.* XIX, 94, in connection with a mime in which 'a large amount of artificial blood was shed'.

69. The discussion about this discovery can be followed by reading V.Tzaferis, 'Jewish Tombs at and near Giv'at ha-Mivtar, Jerusalem', *IEJ* 20, 1970, 18–32; N.Haas, 'Anthropological Observations on the Skeleton Remains from Giv'at ha-Mivtar', ibid., 38–59; Y.Yadin, 'Epigraphy and Crucifixion', *IEJ* 23, 1973, 18–22; V.Moller-Christensen, 'Skeletal Remains from Giv'at ha-Mivtar', *IEJ* 26, 1976, 35–8; H.-W.Kuhn, 'Zum Gekreuzigten von Giv'at ha-Mivtar. Korrektur einse Versehens in der Erstveröffentlichung', *ZNW* 69, 1978, 118–22; 'Der Gekreuzigte von Giv'at ha-Mivtar. Bilanz einer Entdeckung', *Theologia Crucis, Festschrift für Erich Dinkler*, Tübingen 1979, 303–34; Fitzmyer, 'Crucifixion', 494–8; J.Briend, 'Le Crucifié de Jérusalem', *Monde B* 2, 1978, 43 (sketch and illustration). There is insufficient support for Yadin's thesis that Yehohanan will have been crucified head downwards (like St Peter, *Acta Petri* 37; Origen, in Eusebius, *HE* III, 1,2). See Justin, *Apology* I, 35,7 (see also 35,5); *Dial.*97.3, 4; according to Ps.21.17 (LXX).

70. 359–60: '*Primus qui in crucem excucurrerit sed ea lege ut affigantur bis pedes bis bracchia.*'

71. For the question whether the nails were put in the palms see Barbet, *Passion*, 144–7 (the extra arguments drawn from the Turin Shroud are of minimal interest here). In the same sense see also Moller-Christensen, 'Skeletal Remains from Giv'at ha-Mivtar', 36. For the

Gospels, which speak of 'hands', see Luke 24.39, 49; John 20.20, 26, 27. For opinions about the nails for the feet see Holzmeister, '*Crux Domini*', 27–8. For the cross with three nails and its symbolism see J.J.Collins, 'An Exegetical Note: The Crucifixion of Our Lord and Some Medical Data', *CBQ* 12, 1950, 171–2: 171; Blinzler, *The Trial of Jesus*, 265.

72. Justin, *Dial*.91.2; Irenaeus, *Adv.Haer*.II, 24, 2; Tertullian, *Ad nationes*, I, 12,4; *Adv. Marcionem* III, 18.4. In the fragment from Maecenas (c. 70–8 BCE) quoted by Seneca (Ep.101.11), the phrase '*vel acuta si sedeam cruce*' refers only to the punishment of the stake.

73. See the discussion of this in Schmittlein, *Circonstances*, 79–81.

74. This is the date almost universally given to the famous blasphematory graffito on the Palatine, in which the crucified figure with the head of an ass has his feet on the *suppedaneum*; see J.Leclecq, 'Croix et crucifix', *DACL* III/2, 3050–2. The first written attestation is in Gregory of Tours (540–594), *De gloria martyrum* 1, 6, PL 71, 711.

75. For Jesus being nailed while lying on the ground see Epictetus, *Discourses*, III, 26, 22; 'so that in the bath, when you are undressed and stretched out in the position of those who are crucified (*ekteinas seauton hos oi estauromenoi*) you can be rubbed in all directions'. See Firmicus Maternus, *Mathesis*, VI, 31, 38: *patibulo suffixus in crucem tollitur*. The expressions, which are intrinsically equivocal (like *in crucem elevare, ascendere, salire, epibainein tou staurou, anabainein eis stauron*: references in Holzmeister, '*Crux domini*', 19–20) and which some think can hardly be taken to mean being fixed to a complete cross which has set up beforehand, must in reality be understood to describe the raising of the cross-beam (*patibulum*) to the post prepared for it. To establish that we have the texts quoted previously (148 n.12), which show the condemned man bearing the *patibulum* on his shoulders to the place of execution. It should be added that given the dimensions and weight of a post destined to support a human body at a certain height, it is hard to see how someone already weakened by the scourging could have carried a complete cross. Finally it should be noted, with Holzmeister ('*Crux Domini*', 18), that we never find the phrase 'dragging (*syrein*) the cross'; the verbs used always mean 'carry' (*portare, baiulare, pherein, bastazein*). The archaeological details are apparently mute about the technique used for hoisting the *patibulum* with the body to the *stipes* and fixing it there.

76. See above 96f. See also Martial, *Liber spectaculorum* 7, about a representation in which a real criminal, playing the role of the leader of the brigands, was hung from a cross and torn to pieces by a Scottish bear.

See also Suetonius, *Nero,* 29, describing the lewd manias of the emperor in attacking those being crucified while on their crosses. But according to the same historian (*Galba,* 9), Galba, having had a Roman citizen crucified 'telling himself it was to console him and mitigate his torture, ordered that his cross should be changed and that a second one should be set up higher than the others and painted white.' There are other examples in Holzmeister, '*Crux Domini*', 7.

77. Mark 15.27; Matt.27.38; Luke 23.32,33, 39–43; John 19.18.

78. The ban in the Mishnah (Sanhedrin 6, 4) on pronouncing two death sentences (followed by executions) on the same day was not valid in the eyes of Roman law.

79. See Hengel, *Zealots,* 24–30.

80. For example *BJ* II, 125, 228. See Mark 11.7 par. (Jer.7.11, LXX); John 10.1,8; II Cor.11.26 and in the LXX Jer.7.11; Hos.7.1; Obadiah 5.

81. Brown, *John* II, 903, lists, following other authors, turban, *tallit* (outer garment), belt; there is a discussion on the sandals or the *halûq,* jacket (to arrive at the number four).

82. See the bibliography in Blinzler, *The Trial of Jesus,* 255 n.36.

83. For this type of fabric see G.Dalman, *Arbeit und Sitte in Palästina* V, Gütersloh 1937 reprinted Hildesheim 1964, 126–9.

84. Barrett, *John,* 457, notes that 'polyglot notices were probably as common in the Hellenistic period as they are today on continental trains'. He refers to Josephus, *BJ* VI, 125; *Antt.* XIV, 191, and to the bilingual inscriptions of the *Res gestae Divi Augusti.* However, none of these examples relates to an executed man.

85. Against the scepticism of Bultmann (*History,* 284) and Linnemann (*Studien,* 154). To derive this notice from Pilate's question in Mark 15.2, as the latter suggests, is to reverse the order of things. See above, 65. See also J.A.Fitzmyer, *Luke the Theologian: Aspects of His Teaching,* London 1989, 204.

86. John (19.20) remarks that to his knowledge 'many Jews read it', though here perhaps he is exaggerating. For the title 'king of the Jews' see Josephus, *Antt.* XIV, 26 (on an *ex voto* gift, a golden bunch of grapes, from the temple of Jupiter on the Capitol: 'From Alexander, king of the Jews'); XV, 373; XVI, 311. This title does not figure on any of the coins of the Hasmonean or Herodian rulers: see Schürer, *History* I, 211, 217,221, 227, 281, 312 n.85, 343 n.16, 415 n.40. In Matt.2.2 it is the pagan magi who use it. The Gospel of Peter (IV.11) has 'This is the king of Israel', a fully messianic title which the crowds give to Jesus in

John 12.13. It is probable that it was the inscription on the cross which led Christians to recognize the crucified man on Calvary as the Messiah, as is suggested by N.A.Dahl (*The Crucified Messiah and Other Essays*, Minneapolis 1974, 23–33: 23–28) and J.A.Fitzmyer *(Paul and his Theology: A Brief Sketch*, Englewood Cliffs ²1987, 51). It was also this inscription which provoked the gloss of Ps.95 (Hebrew 96).10. This read: 'the Lord has reigned from the tree' (*ho kyrios ebasileusen apo tou xylou*), the first attestation of which is in Justin (*Dial*.73.1).

87. Suetonius, *Caligula*, 32: '*praecedente titulo qui causam poenae indicaret*'; *Domitian*, 10; Dio Cassius 54.3 (about a crucified slave who before his execution was made to cross 'the Forum with an inscription giving the reason why he was going to be put to death'); Eusebius, *HE* V, 1, 44: the martyrdom of Attalus in Lyons: 'He was made to go round the amphitheatre, preceded by a tablet on which had been written in Latin: "This is Attalus the Christian".'

88. According to P.-F.Regard ('Le Titre de la croix d'après les évangiles', *RAr* 5/28, 1928, 95–105), the inscription was trilingual, as John reports; Mark gives only its general tenor; Matthew translates the semitic formula; Luke would be emphasizing the humanity of Christ (?). For G.M.Lee ('The Inscription of the Cross', *PEQ* 100, 1968, 144) Mark would be reproducing the Greek formula which he will have learned from Simon of Cyrene; Luke would be translating the Latin formula; Matthew would have kept the Hebrew (without 'Nazarene') underlying the Greek. These explanations and others of the same kind are fantastic and take no account of the relationship between the Gospels (in this case that between Matthew and Luke, and Mark).

89. Schnackenburg, *Gospel according to John* III, 314.

90. High priests could not have used the expression 'king of the Jews', which expressed contempt for the Jews on Gentile lips, as it did on the inscription.

91. The 'scribes' have been added here probably by Mark, who does not use this category (2.6; 3.22; 12.38–40), whereas the high priests dominate the trial of Jesus (see above, 16).

92. Mark 5.41; 7.34; 14.36; 15.34 (see also 3.17; 7.11; 15.22); without translation, 10.51.

93. See above, 92f., 94.

94. *Elâ(h)î, Elâ(h)î, lema shebaqtanî*, transliterated into Greek. Matthew replaces *Elâ(h)î* (*elôi* according to the local pronunciation) with the Hebrew *Elî*, to facilitate the word-play with the name of the prophet Elijah. The Targum also has *Eli*.

95. Like the Psalmist, Jesus is here thought to feel distress and abandonment by God. But his complaint emanates from faith in a God who remains his God and from whom he has not ceased to expect deliverance. However, that does not mean that we need to tone down this prayer by attributing to Jesus the implicit recitation of the whole Psalm, including the final song of victory (vv.23–32).

96. The solution put forward by M.Rehm ('Eli, Eli, lamma sabachtani', *BZ* NF 2, 1958, 275–8), who thinks that originally Jesus' prayer had 'Eli', as in Matthew, is unfortunate. As we have seen, Matthew in fact is only adapting Mark's text to the subsequent word-play in order to make it less improbable. According to J.Gnilka ('"Mein Gott, mein Gott, warum hast du mich verlassen?" Mk 15,34 par', *BZ* NF 3, 1939, 294–7), Jesus would have prayed in Hebrew, hence the scorn (this explanation is no longer given in Gnilka's commentary on Mark, II, 312–3). The theory of H.Sahlin ('Zum Verständnis von drei Stellen des Markus-Evangelium', *Bib* 33, 1952, 53–66: 62–66); T.Boman ('Das letzte Wort Jesu', *StTh* 17, 1963, 103–19); X.Léon-Dufour (*Face à la mort. Jésus et Paul*, Paris 1979, 160–2), is that Jesus' prayer would have been *Elî attah,* 'It is you, my God', hence the possible confusion with *Eliyyah ta,* 'Elijah, come!' This is pure hypothesis, with no foundation in the texts (despite the presence of *Elî attah* in some psalms: 22.11; 63.2; 118.28; 140.7; add Isa.44.17) and does not explain the transition from a saying appropriate to the context to the quotation of Ps.22.1, which singularly complicates things, from both a narrative and a christological point of view.

97. Basing himself on the variant of the Vetus Latina (k, fourth-fifth century) which has *helion* here, C.H.Turner (*The Gospel According to Mark*, London 1928, 79) suggested that the soldiers saw the prayer of Jesus as a cry to the god Sun. This basis is really too weak!

98. Although the fact of invoking Elijah in distress is not attested before the Gospel of Mark, it has its roots in I Kings 17.8f.; see Jeremias, 'Hêl(e)ias', TDNT 2, 932–3. For the documentation see also [Strack-]Billerbeck IV, 769–79.

99. Mark 15.36; Matt.27.48; Luke 23.36; John 19.28–30.

100. The examples cited by Goguel (*Life of Jesus*, 52–7) establish that drinking vinegar hastens death. In this case, the author comments, 'by giving Jesus a drink, the soldier thinks to hasten his end and the word "Let us see if Elijah will come to his aid" means, "He is going to die instead of being the object of an impossible deliverance"'. But this

comment applies only to the redactions of the Gospels or their sources (see above, 96), and not at the historical level; on the other hand, we do not have to think of pure vinegar (see below).

101. Plautus, *Miles gloriosus*, 836; *Truculentus*, 610; Pliny, *Natural History* 27, 28; Celsus 4, 5 end. Already in the Bible Num.6.3; Ruth 2.14. Add Midrash Ruth 2.14 (133a): 'The harvesters used to dip their bread in vinegar' (*homes*); id., Lev.rabba 34 (13b).

102. John (19.29) speaks of a branch of hyssop, but this is an impossibility, given the nature of this plant. The correction which has replaced it with 'spear' (*hyssos*) is perhaps offering a solution to the problem.

103. See Blinzler, *The Trial of Jesus*, 258–61 and the notes (with bibliography); Barbet, *Passion*, 101–19; Schmittlein, *Circonstances*, 25–43.

104. In writing 'He who has seen bears witness to it' (John 19.36), the evangelist is not necessarily referring to himself. As Dodd comments (*Tradition*, 133–4): 'The natural and straightforward meaning is that someone, not the author, had, to the author's knowledge, witnessed the occurrence, and that it is here recorded according to the testimony of this witness, whoever he may have been.'

105. Tacitus, *Annals* VI, 29: 'A man legally condemned forfeited his estate and was debarred from burial [*sepultura prohibebantur*]; while he who passed sentence upon himself had his celerity so far rewarded that his body was interred and his will respected.' Petronius (*Satyricon*, 11–12) in the spicy and macabre story of the widow of Ephesus, tells us that a guard who by negligence allowed the family of a crucified man to pay their last respects to his body himself expected to be executed.

106. Suetonius, *Augustus* 13; Artemidorus, *Onirocritica* II, 53: 'The crucified one is set on high and feeds many birds of prey . . . those crucified lose their flesh'; Pseudo-Manetho, *Apotelesmatica*, 4: 'they are fixed on it [the cross], nailed there in horrible torments, foul food for the birds of prey and macabre nourishment for the dogs.'

107. Eusebius, *HE* V, 1, 62.

108. Eusebius, *De martyribus Palaestinae* 9, PG 20, 1493–4.

109. *In Flaccum*, 83. See also Tacitus, *Annals* XIV, 12 (acts of clemency by Nero following the burning of Rome).

110. According to John, this sabbath coincided with the Passover, following the peculiar chronology of this Gospel. Josephus (*BJ* IV, 317) criticizes the Idumeans for having thrown out the corpses of the two high priests, Ananus and Jesus, 'without burial, since the Jews attach such

importance to burial that even the malefactors who have been crucified
are taken down and buried before sunset',

111. Origen, *In Matt.*, ser.140, PG 13, 1793; sometimes overnight
and for the following day: *Passio S.Andreae* 12 (Lipsius-Bonnet 2.1,
p.29); Andrew, hanging on the cross for two days, continued to preach.

112. Plautus, *Poenulus*, 886; Origen, *In Matt.*, ser 140, PG 13,
1794: '*secundum consuetudinem Romanorum*'. The crucified man from
the Giv'at ha-Mivtar ossuary (see above, 90f.) had his two tibia and his
right fibula broken at the same level, which suggests that he enjoyed the
same favour as the companions of Jesus.

113. For the spear thrust as a guarantee against possible survival see
Pseudo-Quintilian, *Declamationes maiores*, 6.9: 'They took down the
crosses: the executioner did not forbid the burial of those who had been
struck [by a spear]' (*cruces succiduntur, percussos sepeliri non vetat
carnifex*). See also Holzmeister, '*Crux Domini*', 24. The executioners,
drawn from the auxiliary troops, were 'armed with the *hasta velitaris*,
i.e. a fairly long weapon (2.40 metres), essentially for throwing and of no
use in close combat', notes Schmittlein (*Circonstances*, 89), who refers
to Festus, 28 and Livy, XXXVIII, 20.1.

114. The reference is to John 19.34b–35.

115. The Christ of the passion according to John does not do
miracles, apart from making the guards fall to the ground at his arrest;
the series of miracles ends with the resurrection of Lazarus.

116. Apparently the problem does not apparently arise over the
blood. It is true that a dead body does not bleed, given that the heart has
ceased to pump, but blood can run out of a wound inflicted immediately
after death, especially if the corpse is in a vertical position. The 'water' is
thought of as pericardiac fluid. For this question see Blinzler, *The Trial
of Jesus*, 260; Dodd, *Tradition*, 135–6; Brown, *John* II, 946–8; Barbet,
Passion, 181–3; Schmittlein, *Circonstances*, 85–92.

117. See Mark 15.40–41; Matt.27.55–56; Luke 23.49; John
19.25–27. For their number and their names – a topic which is beyond
our concerns here – see especially R.Bauckham, *Jude and the Relatives
of Jesus in the Early Church*, Edinburgh 1990, 5–19; 'Salome the Sister
of Jesus, Salome the Disciples of Jesus, and the Secret Gospel of Mark',
NT 33, 1991, 243–75.

118. R.Riesner ('Golgota und die Archäologie', *BiKi* 40, 1985, 21–6:
24) envisages them contemplating the scene from the ramparts.

119. On the other hand one could accept that the scene is rooted in
the life of Jesus before the passion. A.Dauer ('Das Wort des Gekreizigten

an seine Mutter und den "Jünger, der er liebte"', *BZ* NF 11, 1967, 222–39: 235; *Die Passionsgeschichte im Johannesevangelium*, StANT 30, Munich 1972, 200), while attributing the creation of the scene and saying of Jesus in John 19.25–27 to the evangellist, does not exclude the possibility of an action on the part of Jesus, who, in other circumstances, could have entrusted his mother to a disciple to whom he was particularly attached.

8. *The Burial*

1. See above, 97f.

2. The amazement of Pilate in Mark 15.44 (this feature is lacking in Matthew and Luke) even contradicts it, since according to John 19.31–32, Pilate had given permission to finish off the crucified men. In fact Joseph's approach in Mark 15.43, also made on the eve of the sabbath, depends on the tradition handed down in John 19.31, but distorts it. C.H.Turner ('The Gospel Narrative of the Lord's Burial', *CQR* 76, 1912, 297) sought to reconcile the two requests: Joseph will have made his at the same time as the Jews. The hypothesis of a double burial of Jesus is more widespread (for the theories of Guignebert, Goguel and Baldensperger see F.-M.Braun, 'La Sépulture de Jésus'). J.S.Kennard Jr, 'The Burial of Jesus', *JBL* 74, 1955, 227–38, offers us another sample: Jesus will have been put in a common ditch by the soldiers in the presence of the women before two o'clock; in the evening Joseph will have buried Jesus in his own tomb. The arbitrariness of this kind of reconciliation of the disparate traditions is only too evident.

3. See Dalman, *Sacred Sites and Ways*, 225–6; F.M.Abel, *Géographie de la Palestine* II, EtB, Paris 1938, 428–9.

4. The type thus depicted is Johannine and betrays a contemporary situation.

5. Scholars sometimes hesitate between the great Sanhedrin of Jerusalem and a local council. But see below, 163f. n.10.

6. The weight of the spices (100 Roman pounds = 32.545 kg) is extravagant, above all if we take account of how light the powders in question were. T.C.de Kruijf ('"More than Half a Hundredweight of Spices" [John 19, 39 NEB]. Abundance and Symbolism in the Gospel of John', *Bijdragen* 43, 1982, 234–9) has thought it possible to remedy this improbability by supposing that the perfumes were in solution and suggesting a measure of capacity, the *kotylê*, which would give twenty litres for Nicodemus' contribution. But we also should not forget the

note in II Chron 16.24, nor the eighty minas of spices burnt at the funeral of Gamaliel the Elder, nor, according to Josephus (*Antt.* XVII, 199), the funeral procession of Herod the Great, which comprised 500 slaves bearing perfumes. M.-J.Lagrange (*Évangile selon saint Jean*, EtB, Paris ⁴1947, 501), who cites other examples from antiquity, is wrong in supposing a copyist's error here. The funerals of the 'king' Jesus (John 18.37) can easily accommodate some extravagances.

7. The Gospel of Peter (VI, 24) supplements here (*elouse*).

8. According to M.-E.Boismard (*Synopse des quatre évangiles en français*, II, Paris 1972, 436), John's source will have said that the 'Jews' took down the body of Jesus from his cross, wrapped it in a shroud and buried it, the action of Joseph of Arimathea corresponding to another tradition. This has the support of the variant, in the plural, in John 19.38c: 'so they came and took it' (instead of 'so he came and took his body'). However, this choice comes up against objections (see J.Murphy-O'Connor, *RB* 81, 1974, 266): it is hard to see the Jews (in reality a delegation of hierocrats) contracting impurity (see Num.19.11) by manipulating a corpse, both historically and in the view of the evangelist, who has spelt out earlier (18.28) that the same figures were scrupulous and 'did not enter the praetorium, so that they might not be defiled, but eat the passover'. Moreover, in John 19.31 the Jews ask Pilate for the bodies to be 'taken away' (*arthôsin*), a passive which stands out from the active in v.38c and relieves the Jews of any direct intervention in the removal of the body. Whatever may be the reason for the two plurals in John 19.38c (in the current text they suggest the collaboration of helpers and could derive from a simple adjustment to the narrative), it cannot be emphasized with the aim of discovering a rival tradition to the one which presents Joseph of Arimathea.

9. The rule is confirmed by Josephus (*BJ* IV, 317) for the period with which we are concerned. He is indignant that the corpses of the high priests are left unburied, 'although the Jews take such care over burial that even those who have been crucified (*anestaurômenous*) by judicial decision are taken down and buried before sunset'. See also *Antt.* IV, 202, 264; Philo, *De spec.legibus* III, 152. It goes without saying that the application of such a rule depended on the Roman power when the execution had taken place on its orders.

10. It is possible that this pious Jew was a member of the Great Sanhedrin and even that he had decided, with his colleagues, to hand Jesus over to Pilate (whatever Luke says, see above, 100), while then proceeding to bury him in faithfulness to the law. But we should not forget the

doubts as to whether the (morning) session of the Sanhedrin was truly legal and, consequently, as to whether all its members were present, or the doubts about the circumstances in which it was held (see above, 50). In any case, it is not very probable that by attributing the entombment of Jesus to the guilty Jews (through Paul as spokesman), the Acts of the Apostles (13.29) is bearing witness to a historical tradition which the Gospel by the same author will have doctored (though this is the view of R.H.Fuller, *The Formation of the Resurrection Narratives*, London and New York 1971, 54–5; Murphy-O'Connor, *RB* 81, 1974, 269; Brown, 'Burial', 244). The difference can easily be explained better in each case by the aims of the writer. Joseph of Arimathea, who buries Jesus, and the 'pious men' who perform the same duty for Stephen (Acts 8.2) bear witness to the sympathy that Jesus and the first Christians were able to arouse among the best in Israel (see also Luke 2.25, 36–37). In Paul's speech at Pisidian Antioch (Acts 13.16–41), the author of Acts is content to schematize the facts, including the burial, in the process of death on which the burial sets its seal, so that the triumph of the resurrection can burst out with all the more splendour (13.29–30).

11. I Kings 13.22; Jer.22.18–19; 26.23. See also I Enoch 98.13.

12. *Antt.* V, 44.

13. *Antt.* IV, 202. Compare Luke 24.16, where we have only stoning (for hanging there is the influence of Deut.21.22–23). On the other hand it is not said that Joseph was ignorant of the rite of second burial, as Büchler, 'L'Enterrement', 88, argues; the context does not call for mention of it in either instance.

14. Sanhedrin 6.5–6. See Büchler, 'L'Enterrement'.

15. Two plots of land, 'one for those who have been beheaded and strangled, the other for those who have been stoned or burned'.

16. This is the fate that it seems we should attribute to the corpse of the crucified man discovered at Giv'at ha-Mivtar, see above, 90f. This second burial for criminals should not be confused with the practice of ossuaries and other analogous usages in the last century of the second temple: see E.M.Meyers, 'Secondary Burials in Palestine', *BA* 33, 1970, 2–29: 17–29; P.Figueras, 'Jewish Ossuaries and Secondary Burial: Their Significance for Early Christianity', *Immanuel* 19, 1984–5, 41–7.

17. It could be objected that the absence of anointing is a necessary element of the story, since it provides in advance the reason for the visit of the women to Jesus' tomb (Mark 16.1 par) and would seem to depend on this last episode, which has hardly any chance of being historical (how could the women have had the idea of anointing, more than

twenty-four hours after death, a body covered in wounds and wrapped in a shroud?). But would the plan to anoint the body have come from the narrator had he known that Jesus had been buried with all due care? Moreover the omission goes against the tendency of the evangelists to emphasize the veneration which stamps Joseph's action; even in Mark, the man clearly acts in accordance with his piety, since he is said to be awaiting the kingdom of God. Rather than being an omission deliberately left by the narrator in view of the following story, this is the remembrance of a rapid burial without any anointing, which will have made it possible to develop the episode of the women at the tomb and give a reason for their visit. M.Shabbat 23, 5: '[On the day of the sabbath] one can do all that is necessary for the dead body: one can anoint it and wash it., take the cushion from under it and put it on the sand to delay decomposition; one can bind up the chin, etc.' For washing the body see also Acts 9.37.

18. For the shroud, we have *sindon* in Mark 15.46 par. Matt.27.59; Luke 23.53; and the same term in Mark 14.52. See Brown ('Burial', 242), who refers to the equally summary burial of Ananias in Acts 5.6.

19. Matthew (27.60) emphasizes that the stone was 'large', a way of preparing for the wonder which is described later (28.2). The elaborate system comprising a cut stone in the form of a disc which was rolled in a groove in front of the tomb cannot be taken to have been established for the period which concerns us. The verb 'roll' (*proskyliein*) employed in the Gospels cannot be used as an argument that the tomb of Jesus had one (thus Kopp, *Itinéraires*, 600); like the Hebrew *golel* (see Dalman, *Sacred Sites and Ways*, 370–1), the Greek verb can be used of a block of stone of any shape which is simply too heavy to be lifted.

20. Shabbat 10.5.

21. See above, 86f.

Index of Subjects

Index of Modern Scholars

Index of References

1. Old Testament

2. New Testament

176 The Trial of Jesus

3. Intertestamental sources

4. Rabbinic sources

5. Graeco–Roman Literature

6. Church Fathers

7. Others